D0843953

Generations

A Collection of Polish and Eastern European
Recipes Handed Down for Over 100 Years
Through Five Generations

MYRA J. GAZIANO

PHOTOGRAPHY BY RINA S. KARLE

GENERATIONS

A Collection of Polish and Eastern European Recipes Handed
Down for Over 100 Years Through Five Generations

Copyright © by Myra J. Gaziano

All rights reserved. Published by the Peppertree Press, LLC.

The Peppertree Press and associated logos are
trademarks of the Peppertree Press, LLC.

No part of this publication may be reproduced, stored in a
retrieval system, transmitted in any form or by any means,
electronic, mechanical, photocopying, recording, or otherwise,
without prior written permission of the publisher and author/illustrator.

Designed by: Parry Design Studio, Inc.

For information regarding permissions, call 941.922.2662
or contact us at our website:
www.peppertreepublishing.com or write to:
The Peppertree Press, LLC
Attention: Publisher
1269 First Street, Suite 7
Sarasota, Florida 34236

ISBN: 9781614935285
Library of Congress Control Number: 2017907118

Printed 2017

Table of Contents

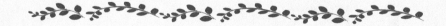

Author's Introduction

Many of the wonderful and delicious recipes found in this cookbook have been handed down for over 100 years, to five generations of women. The recipes are my dowry—a roadmap to my Polish culture and heritage. My great-grandmother, Rose, left me a cherished gift—her spirit and love of cooking as well as her passion to carry on the family traditions she brought with her from Poland. Many of the recipes in this cookbook were recorded from memory, personal "hands-on" instruction from my mother and grandmother, or were sketchily written on the backs of envelopes or scraps of paper. Each recipe was developed, tested and refined into the heavenly aromas and mouthwatering flavors that I grew up with.

Nostalgically reflecting on the past generations of women in my family, I realized that cooking was a cohesive part of their self-actualization. It was one of the few outlets they possessed for creativity and self-expression. Along with the aroma of their kitchens, I can feel the pride and satisfaction they felt when the braided designs on the golden brown *paska* breads were perfect or when the centerpiece of Christmas Eve dinner, a platter of homemade *pieroghi*, brought smiles of anticipated pleasure from those gathered around the dining room table. This was my female mentors' "hands-on" way of telling their story—of who they were, where they came from, and ensuring their treasured traditions would be passed on to a new generation.

Although not physically present, I connect with my mother and grandmother when ritualistically cleaning "the basket" for the Holy Saturday blessing, *Swieconka*, kneading the *paska* bread for Easter, filling the *pieroghi* as part of the *Wigilia* celebration, or ironing the special holiday linens. I lovingly reflect on those women before me whose hands went through the same motions with the same anticipation of the holiday's customs and festivities, who prepared the food rituals in the same spirit, the same time of year, and with the same loving reverence for their seasonal celebrations. It was these women who knew the role food played in keeping a family together and preserving the past. It was these women of little formal education and worldly materials that used food to maintain a bond with their heritage and gave their children an identity as Polish Americans.

Many of the recipes in this book have been prepared and celebrated in America with little change since 1907. The *kuchina polska* of my ancestors was hearty, peasant-style cooking. Although the ingredients may have slightly changed over the years with the availability of food products along with the modern stainless steel appliances, deviation from the special holiday recipes was never an option. Sometimes as I am preparing one of the recipes, I often feel the watchful eyes of my mother or grandmother ensuring that the cutting of the vegetables, the adding of the seasonings and herbs, or the cleaning of the jars for canning are done to their satisfaction. I hear their cooking tips, techniques or anecdotes that were spoken to me often enough that I would never forget them, because they were to be "handed down" to the next generation. And, for this, I feel very blessed and thankful of my heritage.

I hope you enjoy preparing these recipes as well as you will enjoy eating the delicious meals. As the French say "bon appétit" and the Italians "buon appetito," the Polish say… "smacznego" have a tasty meal!

Myra J. Gaziano

A Very Special Thank You

To my amazing daughter, Rina Karle, for creating all of the fabulous photography in this book. Thank you for your constant moral support, creative inspiration, and sharing my love and passion for our heritage. Our work together will ensure that the loving recipes and traditions will be carried on to her children and a new generation.

Foreword

Preserving Polish Culture in America

As many immigrants who crossed the Atlantic, my Polish ancestors made their home in America with little more than hopes and dreams for a new and better life and a fierce determination to succeed. As they settled into their new country, they began to assimilate into the American way of life with its new surroundings, language and culture. At the same time they struggled to maintain continuity with their past and former homeland and preserve many aspects of their "Old World" culture and customs. Creating a Polish ethnicity for themselves and their children in America was attained primarily through their Church and the bonding foods from their ancestral homeland. As most Poles, my maternal great-grandparents, particularly my great-grandmother, were solid and devout Roman Catholics. Being Catholic was a part of their Polish identity, enabling them to intertwine their culture and faith. In other words, the Church provided more than sacred bonds. In fact, it helped to preserve Polish ethnic unity by tying many elements of their life together—their social life, treasured customs and "Old World" traditions, especially those connected to church holidays and rituals such as Easter and Christmas, and weddings, baptisms and first communion celebrations. "Old World" foods were the centerpiece for the solemnly celebrated occasions that carried great significance and symbolism. The church gave them the holidays and religious rituals while ethnic food was the medium to renew and reconnect to the past, savoring former holiday memories with parents and friends left behind, while carving out new traditions yet preserving these "Old World" customs that became uniquely Polish-American.

While I have no formal culinary training, I was compelled to compile this cookbook to share with you this legacy my great-grandmother left, one that has been passed down for over 100 years through five generations of women. This legacy is not only the recipes and ingredients found in this book, but her spirit of joy and reverence for the food that was prepared as a means of preserving her heritage and culture.

Merry Christmas! *Wesolych Swiat Bozego Narodzenia!*
Wigilia, Christmas Eve Supper

As Christians throughout the world anticipate and celebrate the birth of Christ on Christmas Eve, our home was always bustling with the culmination of weeks of cooking preparations for the Polish Christmas Eve supper or *"Wigilia."* *Wigilia* comes from the Latin word vigilare "to await" and literally means "eve." Since Christmas Eve was still technically Advent, the pre-Vatican II Catholic Church mandated that it was a day of strict fast and abstinence, strongly influencing a meatless food ritual. One could wonder how such a wonderful feast evolved without meat. Today, the Church laws have been revised to permit the consumption of meat on Christmas Eve, but a meatless Christmas Eve supper remains the traditional custom in many Polish-American and Eastern European-American homes.

While the variety of items prepared and served for *Wigilia* may have varied regionally throughout Poland, my ancestors brought peasant-type fare that has been incorporated into our traditional meal for generations. Our special holiday dinner consisted of the traditional twelve dishes symbolic for the twelve apostles. The time-honored dishes appearing on our table began with mushroom and sauerkraut soup followed by fried cod and other fishes. The centerpiece of our *wigilia* was the homemade *pieroghi,* the beloved Polish dumpling, with a variety of fillings (potato and cheese, prune, and sauerkraut) and salads and vegetables. The sweet finale required the much-loved nut and poppy seed *kolache, chrusciki, mazurka,* fruits and *krupnik* to raise our glasses to toast *Na Zdrowie* "to our health."

As a way of honoring not only the birth of Christ, but our cherished heritage—always the best china, special holiday linens, shining silver and sparkling crystal enhanced the time-honored family foods that were usually prepared only once a year. After saying grace, with the emotional remembrance of family members who are with us in spirit only, the breaking of *oplatki* with wishes of Merry Christmas and good health and happiness in the New Year are exchanged. The anticipated feasting begins and the traditions that strengthen our ethnic identity, reminding us of our past heritage and "who we are" continue one more year and are passed on to the younger generations.

The Tradition of *Oplatki*

The beautiful centuries-old tradition of *oplatki* originated in Poland, but over the years spread throughout Eastern European countries and across the Atlantic Ocean to America. Today, many Polish–American homes carry on this tradition as part of their Christmas Eve celebration. *Oplatki* is a thin wafer that is very similar in texture to the communion host. The difference is in its appearance. It is usually rectangular in shape, about four-inches by six-inches and is decorated with embossed religious Christmas symbols and pictures such as the Nativity, the Star of Bethlehem or the Christ Child and Blessed Mother.

Oplatki is symbolic of the "breaking of bread." As the family is gathered around the *wigilia* table and grace is said, usually the oldest person present or the head of the hosting family breaks a piece off of the wafer, then passes the oplatki wafer to the person next to him or her to break off a piece. The passing of the wafer accompanies a hug and or a kiss as well as an exchange of best wishes. "Merry Christmas and Happy New Year" is typical in our home, but any heart-felt expression is appropriate.

With all of the hustle and bustle that the Christmas holiday season brings, this emotional and heart-warming moment provides the opportunity to truly reflect on the purpose of the festivities as well as the loved ones who are joined together around the *wigilia* table to celebrate Christ's birth.

Our Traditional Family Christmas Eve *Wigilia* Menu

Sauerkraut and Mushroom Soup • *Pieroghi* with Various Fillings
Fried Cod with *Sos Tatarski* • Dilled Shrimp
Roasted Root Vegetables and Salads
Desserts: *Kolache, Chrusciki, Mazurka, Krupnik*

Christmas

Christmas Eve *Wigilia* Sauerkraut and Mushroom Soup

Pieroghi

Pieroghi Fillings

Dilled Shrimp

Fried Cod with *Sos Tatarski*

Noodles with Poppy Seed *Kluski Z Makiem*

Roasted Root Vegetables with Herbs

Povitica

Holiday *Povitica* Coffee Cake

Mazurka

Kolache

Chrusciki

Krupnik

Christmas Eve *Wigilia* Sauerkraut and Mushroom Soup

In Poland, this recipe used borowiki mushrooms that were very abundant in the forests. The borowiki variety of mushrooms gave the soup a deeper color and a richer, nutty flavor. That is why I added the baby portabellas to this recipe, to try to reproduce the color and flavor.

This recipe is for a large group, but can easily be divided in half. Leftover soup also freezes well.

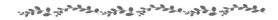

Ingredients:

4 pounds sauerkraut (I like the refrigerated
    type in plastic bags)
2 pounds fresh mushrooms sliced (I like
    to mix baby portabellas and white cremini
    mushrooms)
2 large white onions, chopped (about 4 cups)
44 ounces chicken stock (1 quart plus
    12 ounces)
1½ sticks butter
1 teaspoon sugar
½ cup flour
4 tablespoons parsley, coarsely chopped
Salt and pepper to taste

Directions:

Put sauerkraut in a colander in the sink and rinse well with cold water and let drain for a few minutes. Put the sauerkraut in a pot and just barely cover with chicken stock. Let sauerkraut come to a low boil and cook over medium heat for about 45-60 minutes, then add the mushrooms, parsley and salt and pepper. Continue to simmer for about another 30 minutes before you add the *zaprashka*.

Meanwhile, make your *zaprashka*, a Polish roux used to thicken and flavor this soup. Melt the butter in a large skillet. Add the onions, salt and pepper, and sugar and sauté the onions until they become caramelized. You want the onions to reach a deep golden color. Add the flour to the onions and cook, stirring constantly for 2-3 minutes until the mixture turns light brown.

Remove from the heat.

After your sauerkraut and mushrooms in the soup are soft (about 1½ hours total cooking time), add 2-3 cups or dippers of the soup into the *zaprashka* stirring constantly until well blended and the flour is smooth. This will thin out the roux a little before adding to the soup. Then add all of the flour mixture to the soup stirring constantly until well blended. The *zaprashka* is the thickening agent for the soup. Let the soup cook for about another 10 minutes stirring frequently, taste and re-season if necessary.

Note: I have made this soup a few days in advance. Just reheat on Christmas Eve. If you like a thinner soup, add a little water or chicken broth.

Pieroghi

In a family of good cooks, all of my aunts had their own "best" version of *pieroghi*. I've had the opportunity to sample all of them and included two of the family's favorites, my grandmother's and my Aunt Doris' recipes. Both are excellent!

For our *Wigilia* celebration I usually make an assortment of pieroghi including potato and cheese, sauerkraut, and prune. But if I make only one type of filling, I think the potato and cheese goes best with the soup and fish for Christmas Eve.

My Grandmother and Mom's *Pieroghi* Dough

Ingredients:

5 cups all purpose flour
Dash of salt
2 large eggs, slightly beaten
1 cup sour cream
2 tablespoons melted butter
2 teaspoons vegetable oil

Directions to make the dough:

Wisk together all of the wet ingredients: eggs, sour cream, melted butter and oil. Gradually stir in the flour and salt. Mix well until the dough comes together. The dough will be sticky. Turn out the dough on a well-floured wood board and knead for about 4-5 minutes until the dough is smooth and elastic. Form the dough into two balls and let rest, covered for 10-15 minutes. Then roll the dough and fill with any of the following fillings. This recipe makes about 2-3 dozen *pieroghi*, depending on the size you make them.

Aunt Doris' *Pieroghi* Dough

Ingredients:

4 cups all purpose flour
Dash of salt
2 large eggs, slightly beaten
1 cup of hot water with 2 tablespoons melted butter

Directions to make the dough:

Add flour and salt to a large bowl. Make a well in the center of the flour and add ½ of the wet ingredients. Begin incorporating the flour, then adding the remaining wet ingredients. Mix well until the dough comes together. The dough will be sticky. Turn out the dough on a well-floured wood board and knead for about 4-5 minutes until the dough is smooth and elastic. More flour may need to be added while kneading. Form the dough into two balls and let rest under an inverted bowl for 20 minutes. Then roll the dough and fill with any of the following fillings. This recipe makes about 2-3 dozen *pieroghi*, depending on the size you make them.

Directions to assemble the *Pieroghi*:

On a floured board, roll one of the dough balls about 1/8 inch thick. Keep the rest of the dough covered.

With a 3-4 inch cookie cutter or drinking glass, cut the dough in circles. To make a pieroghi, take a circle of dough, fill it with 1 heaping tablespoon of filling. Try to put the filling to one side of the circle of dough, rather than in the center. Then gently stretch the dough over the filling and press together to close by crimping the dough using your thumb and forefinger or you can use the tines of a fork to seal the pieroghi.

Please Note: When closing the dough over the filling, try to let all of the air out prior to sealing the pieroghi. Pieroghi can be frozen and stored for several months.

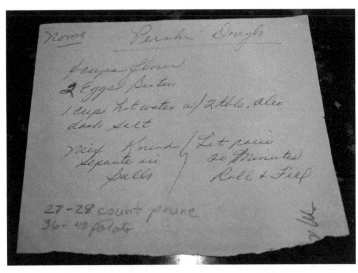

Cooking the *Pieroghi*:

Add each pieroghi individually to a large pot of boiling water that has been salted. Don't overload the pot! Let the pieroghi boil for about 5-6 minutes and when they float to the top of the water they are ready to take out of the water. Carefully remove them from the water with a slotted spoon or wire basket type utensil and place in a shallow serving bowl or plate. Drizzle with melted butter and caramelized chopped onions and fresh ground pepper.

Pieroghi Fillings

Potato and Cheese

Ingredients:

5 pounds Idaho potatoes
10 ounces shredded longhorn cheese
Salt and fresh ground pepper to taste

Directions:

Peel and cut the potatoes in quarters and boil until tender. Drain well and mash the potatoes, then add the rest of the ingredients.

Prune Filling

Ingredients:

2 large boxes of quality pitted prunes
Water

Directions:

Coarsely chop the prunes and put in a pot and cover with water. Cook over medium heat until the prunes are soft and the water has evaporated. Mash prunes by hand or in a food processor for a few seconds. I like my prune filling a little thick and chunky and not finely pureed.

(Continued)

(Continued)

Sauerkraut Filling

Ingredients:

2 one pound bags of sauerkraut

1 large onion, chopped

2 tablespoons olive oil or butter (I prefer oil)

Directions:

Rinse and drain the sauerkraut well. Heat oil in a skillet, add onions and cook until slightly caramelized. Season the onions with salt and pepper. Add sauerkraut to onion mixture and cook about 25 minutes until sauerkraut becomes soft and golden in color.

Note: This may seem like too little oil, but you want as little as possible so that no oil seeps out onto the dough because the oil will prevent the dough from sealing together when you crimp the pieroghi.

Note: I find it easier to make each filling a day or two in advance and work with it cold out of the refrigerator. Each filling makes about 5 dozen pieroghi but the recipe can be divided in half. For 5 dozen pieroghis, double the dough recipe.

Dilled Shrimp

This recipe was added as a lighter alternative to the *Wigilia* menu, for those who cannot eat fried foods. Great as an appetizer!

Ingredients:

1½ pounds extra large or jumbo shrimp that have been cleaned, deveined, cooked and cooled

2 large lemons, juice and zest

½ cup extra virgin olive oil

2 tablespoons fresh dill, chopped

½ cup fresh parsley, chopped

3 tablespoons capers (optional)

Salt and pepper to taste

Directions:

Boil the shrimp, drain, and let cool. In a small bowl, add oil, salt and pepper, lemon juice and zest and mix well. (If you prefer more lemon, add it.) Add the remaining ingredients and lightly toss. Chill well and serve.

Fried Cod with *Sos Tatarski*

Ingredients:

4 pounds fresh Alaskan cod
2 cups flour for breading, seasoned with
 kosher sea salt, fresh ground pepper, and
 2 teaspoons of Hungarian sweet paprika
Oil for frying the fish (I prefer olive oil)

Directions:

Cut the cod into individual serving pieces. Dip the cod into the seasoned flour and coat well on all sides. Put the breaded cod on a tray covered with waxed paper. (This can be done hours in advance of frying and can be stored uncovered or loosely covered in the refrigerator.) Heat oil in a large skillet and when hot add fish and fry on medium-high heat until lightly brown on both sides. Put the cod on paper towel to drain and season with additional sea salt. Then transfer to a serving platter and serve immediately.

Note: the amount of cod can be adjusted accordingly, this recipe is for a crowd.

Tartar Sauce *Sos Tatarski*

Ingredients:

½ cup mayonnaise
½ cup sour cream
¼ cup finely-chopped sweet gherkin pickles
2 teaspoons pickle brine
2 teaspoons finely-chopped fresh dill
¼ teaspoons salt

Directions:

Blend mayonnaise and sour cream together. Add the other ingredients and mix well.

Noodles with Poppy Seed *Kluski Z Makiem*

Eastern Europeans love poppy seeds and have incorporated them into many recipes from breads to desserts.

Since poppy seeds are symbolic of prosperity, they are frequently incorporated into the *Wigilia* meal. The original recipe used poppy seeds that were soaked for many hours and then sweetened with honey, but this recipe has been adapted using a can of poppy seed filling that I think is better.

Ingredients:

1 pound wide noodles (I like bow tie shaped pasta)
1 12-ounce can poppy seed filling such as Solo
¾ cup sour cream
4 tablespoon butter
1 teaspoon vanilla
½ cup golden raisins (optional)
Juice and zest of 1 lemon
Salt to taste

Directions:

Cook noodles according to package directions (do not over-cook), drain and place in a bowl. Add butter and mix to melt through the noodles, then add sour cream, salt, and raisins.

In a separate saucepan, add the can of poppy seed filling, vanilla, lemon juice and zest. Mix well and heat mixture. Add to noodles and mix well. Serve warm.

Roasted Root Vegetables with Herbs

Not only are root vegetables popular in Eastern European cooking, they are also loaded with nutrition and are usually inexpensive. During the winter months when many vegetables are not available, try this recipe using any combination of root vegetables that you like. Any of the following root vegetables are especially good for roasting and may be used for this recipe: carrots, beets, parsnips, rutabagas, baby turnips, sweet potatoes, fingerling potatoes, onions, shallots, leeks or red potatoes.

Ingredients:

6 large carrots, scraped and cut into
  two-inch pieces
4 medium beets, peeled and cut in half
6 red new potatoes, cut in half or quarters
  depending on the size
1 large sweet potato, cut into two-inch
  pieces
1 large white onion, peeled and cut in
  quarters
1 large red onion, peeled and cut in
  quarters
4 large parsnips, scraped and cut into
  two-inch pieces
½ cup olive oil
2 tablespoons fresh rosemary, finely chopped
2 tablespoons fresh dill, chopped
Salt and pepper to taste

Directions:

It is important that all of the vegetables are about the same size to ensure that they will all be cooked at the same time. Place all of the vegetables in a large baking dish or two (not to crowd the vegetables), drizzle olive oil, toss with your hands to evenly coat, add rosemary and generously season with salt and pepper. Place pan in a preheated 400-degree oven and roast for about 45 minutes until the vegetables are tender and brown in some spots. Remove from oven, arrange on a serving dish and sprinkle with dill.

Povitica

Povitica has been adopted by many Eastern European countries. It is a very thinly-rolled yeast dough that is filled with a variety of different fillings such as poppy seed, nut, apricot, and so on. The beauty of this dessert is the swirls that are created from placing the dough in an "S" shape in the pan.

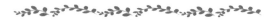

Ingredients to activate yeast:

2 packages dry yeast
½ cup warm water (100-110 degrees)
2 teaspoons granulated sugar

Ingredients for dough:

2 cups whole milk
7-8 cups flour
4 large eggs
½ cup butter
¾ cup granulated sugar
2 teaspoon salt

Ingredients for nut filling:

2 pounds finely ground walnuts
4 cups sugar
2 cups whole milk
1 cup butter
3 large eggs

Directions:

First activate the yeast by adding the yeast to the water, then stir in the sugar. Set aside the mixture.

Put milk into a sauce pot and scald, then let cool to warm (about 100 – to 110 degrees) and then add the yeast mixture. Melt the butter and let cool. Beat the eggs and add the sugar. Add yeast mixture to the eggs and then add the cooled butter. Place all the wet ingredients in a large bowl, large enough to hold the flour. Gradually, add the flour about one cup at a time until all the flour has been incorporated. After the dough is well mixed, you can transfer it onto a floured board to knead until the dough becomes smooth. If the quantity of dough is too large to handle, divide it into two amounts to knead. After kneading the

14

dough, form it into two balls, then put the balls into a buttered large bowl, cover it with plastic wrap and a clean cloth, and let it rise till doubled for about 60 minutes. This dough recipe makes 2 *povitica* rolls.

Next you will want to make the nut filling by adding the walnuts and sugar in a large bowl. Heat the milk and butter until it boils and pour it over the walnuts. Add the beaten eggs and mix very well. Let cool. (If mixture becomes too thick to spread, add a little milk.)

Take one of the dough balls and begin rolling on a floured board in a rectangle shape until the dough is very thin and opaque. If you think it is thin enough, it probably isn't. Keep rolling. Then spread ½ of the filling evenly all over the dough. Beginning with the edge of the dough nearest you, roll the dough away from you in a jelly roll fashion and pinch the seam together well. Cut off each end and then carefully place your roll into a well-buttered loaf pan in the shape of an "S." Then repeat with remaining dough. Brush the *povitica* with egg wash and put two pats of butter on the top. Cover the pans loosely with plastic wrap and let rise for about 30 minutes. Bake the *povitica* in a preheated oven at 350 degrees for 30-45 minutes. If your *povitica* is getting too brown, cover it with foil. Let cool for about 10 minutes before removing from the pan.

Holiday *Povitica* Coffee Cake

My son-in-law's love for cinnamon rolls inspired me to adapt this classic recipe into a coffee cake using commercial hot roll mix. Who would not welcome a few shortcuts during the Christmas holidays or anytime, especially when there is no shortcut in taste! This can be made in advance and frozen to be enjoyed on Christmas morning or anytime.

Ingredients:

1 box of Hot Roll Mix (follow directions for cinnamon rolls)
2 heaping tablespoons cinnamon
8 ounces butter well softened
2 ounces cold butter
1 cup sugar
1½ cups pecans, chopped rather fine
2 tablespoons orange zest (optional)

Directions for Coffee Cake:

Mix sugar and cinnamon together. Prepare roll mix according to the directions for cinnamon rolls. Roll dough approximately into a 24 by 18 inch rectangle. The most difficult part of this recipe is rolling the dough as thin as possible to where you can almost see through it. The rule of

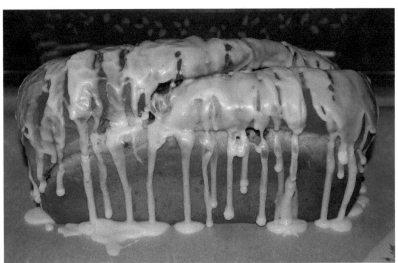

thumb is "when you think the dough is thin enough, roll it a little thinner." Once the dough is rolled, gently slather it with softened butter to the very end of the dough. Sprinkle the sugar and cinnamon

(Continued)

(Continued)

mixture over the butter to the end of the dough, then top with the nuts. Cut the two ounces of cold butter in thin slices and randomly put on the top of the sugared dough. Beginning with the edge of the dough nearest you, roll the dough away from you in a jelly roll fashion and pinch the seam together well. Cut off each end and then carefully place your roll into a well buttered bread-loaf pan in the shape of a "S." Bake in a preheated 375-degree oven for 10 minutes. Reduce heat to 350 and continue baking for 40-45 minutes. If the coffee cake becomes too brown, cover with foil and continue baking. Remove from oven and let sit in pan for five minutes then remove the cake from the pan onto a cooling rack. When cool drizzle with icing.

Icing Glaze

Ingredients:

1½ cups confectionery sugar
2-3 tablespoons half-half
½ teaspoon vanilla

Directions:

Place confectionery sugar in a bowl. To the confectionery sugar slowly add 2 teaspoons of half-half and begin beating with a wooden spoon the sugar. Beat the vanilla into the mixture. If the icing is too thick, add more half-half until it has the consistency that you can drizzle on your coffee cake. Drizzle the icing on the coffee cake and let set.

Mazurka

If asked what is *mazurka*, many may respond that it is a lively Polish folk dance resembling the rhythm of a polka. And that is correct! But it is also a wonderful and very versatile flat bar-type pastry, somewhat between a short-bread and a pound cake. On top of the buttery cake like "crust," the toppings are limitless and often reflect the fruit that is in season—cherries, blueberries, plums or apricot *lekvar*.

This recipe has been reinvented over the years and coconut has been added to the original version. This mazurka recipe includes a "winter apricot *lekvar* fruit" and a "summer fresh blueberry *beserka* filling." But other dried or fresh fruit fillings or preserves may be used. This dessert is so easy, but so delicious!

Ingredients:

1½ cups flour

⅛ teaspoon salt

1½ sticks cold butter, cubed

1 cup firmly packed brown sugar

½ cup shredded coconut plus ⅓ cup for topping

½ cup chopped walnuts

¾ cup oats (not instant or quick) plus ⅓ cup for topping

1 cup apricot *lekvar* (see recipe in this book) or one can of apricot filling

Directions:

In the food processor (or you can use a pastry cutter), add flour, sugar, salt, butter and pulse until the mixture is well mixed. Add coconut, oatmeal, and nuts and pulse for 2–3 seconds just to blend.

In a buttered 8-inch square pan, add about 3 cups of the mixture. Press the mixture into the bottom of the pan, using your fingers or the back of a spoon. Spread the apricot filling over the butter mixture.

For the crumb topping, use the remaining butter mixture and add the extra oats and coconut and blend well. Evenly distribute the crumb topping over the top and gently press down.

Bake in a pre-heated oven at 325 degrees for 35-40 minutes. Let mixture cool completely in the pan before cutting.

Note: If you double this recipe it is recommended to use two 8-inch square pans. It keeps the bottom crispy.

Dried Apricot *Lekvar* Filling

Coarsely chop one box of dried apricots, place in saucepan and soak for a few hours in about 1½ cups of water. Cook over medium heat, stirring frequently until the fruit becomes soft and somewhat melts. Add more water as needed. Add 1 cup of granulated sugar. Stir until smooth and let cool completely. This filling can be made and refrigerated or even frozen in advance.

Fresh Blueberry *Beserka* Filling

Ingredients:

1½ cups fresh blueberries

2 tablespoons granulated sugar

¼ cup of blueberry liqueur or Chambord

1 tablespoons cornstarch

Directions:

Place all of the ingredients in a sauce pan and cook over medium heat for about 5-8 minutes until the berries thicken. Cool completely before using.

Kolache (Small cookie type with cream cheese dough)

This particular *kolache* recipe that does not include yeast is made for Christmas in our home. I like to fill them with a variety of fillings of canned cherry pie filling, poppy seed, pineapple preserves with nuts or apricot. To me, dusted with powder sugar, they reflect Christmas. Double this recipe if you want them for Christmas!

Ingredients:

8 ounces cream cheese
1 cup unsalted butter
2¾ cups flour
¼ teaspoon salt
1 cup powdered sugar plus more for dusting
½ cup granulated sugar
2 cans of cherry pie filling, poppyseed filling,
    or the following recipe for apricot filling

Directions:

The butter and cream cheese must be at room temperature. Beat butter and cheese with an electric mixer and then gradually add the flour and mix until just combined. Form the dough into two balls, wrap in plastic wrap and refrigerate for at least 1 hour. Roll the dough on a board that has been dusted with equal parts of ½ cup granulated sugar and ½ cup powdered sugar. The dough should be rolled about ¼-inch thick. Cut into 3-inch squares. I made a 3-inch template out of a hard piece of plastic and use it as a guide so my cookies will be uniform in size. Fill each square with filling. I put two cherries from the can with a little of the pie filling thickening (or a teaspoon of apricot filling). Then bring one point over the filling and pinch to close. To ensure that the overlapped dough does not open during baking, use a little water on the overlap dough and pinch well. Place *kolache* on a lightly greased baking sheet and bake at 375 degrees for about 17 minutes. When cool, dust with powdered sugar. This recipe makes about 4-5 dozen cookies.

Note: If dough becomes too soft to work with, refrigerate it for about 15 minutes.

Apricot Filling

Ingredients:

10 oz. box dried apricots, coarsely chopped
1 cup water or more if the filling becomes too dry
½ cup sugar or more (apricots vary in sweetness)
¼ cup of orange marmalade (optional)

Directions:

Put the apricots, sugar and water into a saucepan and cook over medium heat until the apricots soften and all of the water is absorbed. You may need to add more water. Stir frequently. Transfer to a food processor, add marmalade and pulse until smooth. If mixture is too thick you can thin the apricots with a little orange juice or water.

Chrusciki

Chrusciki loosely translated in Polish means "cookie," and is associated with pre-Lenten carnival festivities in Poland. These delicate and festive "Polish angel wings" are traditionally found on ethnic Polish-American tables for Christmas, at weddings and other special occasions.

Ingredients:

2¾ cups all purpose flour
½ teaspoon salt
1 tablespoon softened unsalted butter
⅓ cup granulated sugar
¼ cup sour cream
3 eggs and 2 egg yolks
Zest from one lemon
1 teaspoon lemon extract
1 teaspoon orange extract
Vegetable oil for frying the dough
2 cups powdered sugar

Directions:

Mix together dry ingredients: flour, salt and baking powder. In a mixer, beat butter and sugar until fluffy, beat in sour cream, eggs, flavorings and zest. Add flour mixture and mix by hand until just combined. Knead dough and divide dough into two balls. Cover dough with a cloth and let rest for 30 minutes. Roll dough to about ⅛ inch thick on a floured board. With a pastry wheel or knife, cut the dough into 4" long by 1½-inch wide strips. Cut the ends in a diagonal and make a slit with your knife in the center of each piece of dough. Gently pull one end of the dough through the slit to form a bow shaped cookie. Drop into the hot oil (about 375 degrees) and fry for about 2 minutes or until lightly browned on both side. Remove from the oil with a slotted spoon and let drain on paper towel. Transfer to another sheet pan and dust with powdered sugar.

Krupnik

This honey-flavored drink is a Polish liqueur that is served with desserts or by itself on Christmas. It can be made or purchased commercially but homemade and hot during the holiday season is a Polish family tradition like eggnog.

Note: the aroma of cinnamon, cloves and orange will make your home smell festive!

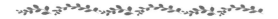

Ingredients:

1½ cups orange honey
⅔ cups water
1 vanilla bean (scrape the beans from the pod with a
    knife)
½ teaspoon nutmeg
6 cinnamon sticks
2 whole cloves
Rind from ½ lemon and orange
1 bottle of good quality vodka (800 ml.)

Directions:

In a large sauce pot, mix honey and water, then add all of the ingredients except the vodka. Bring to a boil and let simmer for 5 minutes. Remove the sauce pot away from the stove and add the vodka. Return to the stove to heat for 1-2 minutes. Serve warm. *Krupnik* can be stored for a week in a cool place.

Paczki Day – Ash Wednesday Tradition

Paczki – "Jelly Filled Doughnut" Tradition

Many countries, cultures and ethnic groups have their version of a doughnut. Poles have elevated this confection to a specially recognized day, "*Paczki* Day." *Paczki* literally means "package" and this package has a wonderful jelly surprise inside.

My grandmother made these delicacies and filled them with her homemade grape jelly and then sprinkled them with granulated sugar. They are delectable! Tradition dictates the preparation of *paczki* on Fat Tuesday or the day before lent begins on Ash Wednesday. This was the last sugary treat before the 40-day fast of Lent, so you really made the most of this last sweet indulgence.

Jelly Filled Doughnuts *Paczki* Recipe

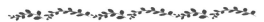

Ingredients for Sponge:

1 cup all purpose flour
2 packages dry yeast
1 tablespoon sugar
2 tablespoons warm water
1 cup lukewarm milk

Directions for Sponge:

Dissolve both packets of yeast in the warm water, then stir in the sugar. In a mixing bowl combine the warm milk and flour. Then add the yeast mixture and blend. Cover with a clean towel until it doubles in size, about an hour.

Ingredients for Dough:

5 eggs
½ cup granulated sugar
¼ cup soft butter
6 cups all purpose flour
1½ teaspoon salt
1 shot whiskey

Directions for the dough:

Beat eggs and sugar until fluffy and then the salt, butter, and whiskey, and mix well. Add the sponge mixture and blend well. Gradually add the flour and lightly knead in the bowl. Cover with a cloth and let rise about 1 hour until the dough doubles in size.

(Continued)

(Continued)

Divide the dough into 2 balls (one ball will be the bottom of the donuts and the second ball will be for the top of the donut). Roll the first ball which will be the bottoms of your donuts on a lightly floured board to about ½ inch thickness and cut in three inch circles. Repeat this process with the second ball of dough for the tops of your donuts. You want to have an equal amount of tops and bottoms. Drop 1 teaspoon of jelly in the center of half of your rounds and brush the edges of the rounds with jelly with water and top with the remaining rounds. Seal the edges well so the jelly does not seep out when frying. Cover the *paczki* with a cloth for about 20 minutes to rest. Fry the *paczki* in 350-degree vegetable oil until lightly brown on both sides. Carefully remove from the oil onto paper towel. Dust with granulated sugar, let cool and enjoy!

Happy Easter! *Wesolych Swiat Wesolego Alleluja!*

Celebrating Christ's glorious resurrection and the renewal of the Christian faith on Easter has always been my favorite holiday. With great anticipation and joy, I welcomed the end of Lent with its forty days of fasting, spring flowers, new Easter outfits, the coloring of Easter eggs, chocolate bunnies, and of course the sacred religious rituals that influenced the rhythm of our home and the weeklong preparations of traditional Polish holiday food during Holy Week.

One of these traditions, and the most beautiful and revered Eastern European tradition that is celebrated among every Slavic group, is the blessing of food "*swieconka*" on Holy Saturday. (Swieconka comes from the word *swiecic* which means to bless.) Our *Swieconka* preparations begin on Holy Thursday with the washing of the special basket that is used only for this occasion. After the

basket is dried from its washing, the bottom is lined with heavy duty foil so the dripping from the food does not saturate and stain the wicker. The baskets are often decorated with pastel ribbons, greenery or spring flowers. The centerpiece of the basket is my *paska* bread, prominently centered. The lamb butter mold with whole cloves for eyes is frozen ahead of time so it will not melt in the warm weather. The bases of the meats as well as the *kolache* are wrapped with foil. This enables them to stand upright as well as keeps them clean and protected. The basket is then covered with a special white linen cloth embroidered with symbols of the Resurrection before taken to Church to be blessed.

On Holy Saturday, the basket is filled with a "sampling" of the traditional food items that were lovingly prepared throughout the week. The food items to be blessed often vary among families and may be based on the ethnic region that the family is from, food preferences and of course the family's financial means. My basket includes a homemade *paska*, a round sweet rich yeast bread, whose top is encircled with three strips of braided dough to signify the Three Persons of the Holy Trinity and decorated with a cross and other

(Continued)

(Continued)

religious symbols; apricot and nut rolls called *kolache; baranek,* a butter molded in the shape of a lamb; *cwikla,* horseradish mixed with grated red beets; a homemade egg custard-type cheese called *cirek;* and decorated hard boiled eggs, kielbasa, ham, salt, wine and other "sweet" delicacies fill the basket to the brim.

After hours of meditating on Christ's Passion during the Adoration and Stations of the Cross on Good Friday, taking the basket to be blessed is always a joyous and festive occasion. With great pride and reverence, each family places their basket on the altar or down the center aisle of the Church in anticipation for the "blessing" to begin. Visually, the baskets are a sight to behold, but it is the aroma in the air filled with scents of ham, kielbasa, and fresh *paska* bread that is overwhelmingly wonderful and makes my mouth water just thinking about it. Traditionally, the priest ceremoniously sprinkles each basket with holy water and prays the "blessing" rituals. The basket is then taken home to be enjoyed on Easter morning for breakfast.

After mass on Easter Sunday morning, the celebration begins, breaking the fast of the 40 days of Lent. "The basket" is placed on a beautiful tablecloth with the following prayer:

Bless us and this food of our first Easter meal.
May we who gather at the Lord's table,
Continue to celebrate the joy of His Resurrection
and be admitted to His heavenly banquet.
Amen.

After grace, we feast on blessed *paska* bread, butter, eggs, cheese and other foodstuffs from the basket. There is always something about the blessed foods that makes everything taste even better! My mother said it was because the food was "blessed."

Historically, the tradition of no hot foods evolved because "no smoke" was permitted by the Roman Catholic Church on the feast of the Resurrection. As a result, hot meals could not be served and *Swieconka* cleverly evolved.

Swieconka, a centuries old tradition, can be enjoyed by the whole family!

Swieconka "Easter Basket Blessing" Preparation

Items that go into a traditional Polish Easter *Swieconka* Basket and the symbolism of each item:

- Ham and Kielbassi – symbolic of God's abundance, mercy and generosity as well as great joy in the Resurrected Christ
- *Paska* Bread – symbolic for Jesus Christ who is the "Bread of Life"
- *Baranek* Lamb-Molded Butter – symbolic for the sacrificial Lamb of God, to remind us of the goodness of Christ
- Decorated Easter Eggs/*Pisanki* – symbolizes new life, rebirth and Christ's Resurrection from the tomb
- White Linen Cloth – often embroidered with symbols of Christ or signs of Easter is used to cover the food when taken to the church; symbolic for the shroud that wrapped Christ's body

- Horseradish - symbolizes the bitter herbs of Passover and the bitter suffering of Jesus on the cross
- *Cwilka* – (horseradish mixed with beets) symbolizes Christ's Passion that is sweetened through the Resurrection
- Salt – symbolizes that which preserves us from corruption and adds zest to life
- Candle – symbolizes Christ the Light of the World
- *Kolache* or other confections – symbolizes the sweetness of eternal life
- *Cirek* – an egg custard-type cheese shaped into a ball, is a symbol of the moderation Christians should have at all times

Our Family's Traditional Polish Easter Buffet Menu

Baked Ham • Stuffed Cabbage Rolls *Golabki* • Easter Cheese *Cirek*
Beet and Horseradish Relish *Cwilka* • Pickled Beets and Eggs • Spring Vegetables *Polonaise*
Paska Bread • Lamb Molded Butter *Baranek* • Easter *Babka Wielkanocna*
Easter Cheese *Kolache* • Lamb Cake

Happy Easter *Wesolych Swiat! Weslego Alleluja!*

Our traditional Easter Menu:

Easter Cheese *Cirek*

Paska Bread

Horseradish with Beets *Cwikla*

Mom's Stuffed Cabbage Rolls *Golabki* or *Halupki*

Beet Pickled Eggs

Mickey's Easter Cottage Cheese *Kolache/Kolaczki*

Vegetables *Polonaise Jarzyny po Polsku*

Easter Cheese *Cirek*

This homemade cheese has a custard-like flavor with a hint of sweetness. It is made only at Easter to be included in the *Swieconka* basket. After cooking, it is formed into a round ball shape with cheese cloth and chilled. There is no other cheese that says Easter to me. It goes so well with *paska* bread, *cwikla*, ham, and pickled eggs.

Ingredients:

12 eggs
1 quart whole milk
1 teaspoon salt
1 tablespoon granulated sugar
1 teaspoon vanilla
Pinch of nutmeg

Directions:

Step 1

Place a colander in the sink and double line it with cheesecloth. Let a little hang over the colander. (You will pour the cheese mixture into this cheesecloth to drain and mold the cheese.)

Step 2

Beat eggs well (I use an electric mixer). Put all ingredients in a sauce pot. Do not cook over a direct flame, use a double boiler or put a griddle under the pot so the milk will not burn or scorch. Cook over medium heat stirring frequently for about 30 minutes until mixture curdles.

Step 3

Pour hot mixture into the strainer lined with cheese cloth. Let mixture drain well. Bring together the cheesecloth to form a ball and squeeze the top of the cheesecloth tight to remove the water. Shape the cheesecloth in a ball, tie to the kitchen sink faucet and let the cheesecloth and cheese mixture drain for about 2 hours. Cover with a moist towel and refrigerate. After chilled, gently remove cheesecloth and cover with plastic wrap until ready to use. (Keep it wrapped in the refrigerator until it is placed in your basket to be blessed.)

Paska Bread

    Paska (meaning Easter) is the cherished Easter bread that is traditionally baked in Eastern European countries, including Poland, Ukraine and Slovakia, as well as in the United States. Paska is believed to have originated in Poland or the Ukraine. It is a sweet rich bread made with butter, eggs and sugar and typically baked in a round pan. To create the bread's shiny glaze, an egg wash is brushed on the dough before going into the oven. The top of paska is often decorated with religious symbols, particularly with crosses and braids comprised of three pieces of dough, symbolic for the Holy Trinity. My family's *paska* was always baked in a deep round pan and elaborately decorated with a large braid circling the perimeter of the bread and a cross in the center symbolizing the Resurrection of Jesus. *Paska* is the centerpiece of our *Swieconka* basket of foods to be "blessed" and eaten at Easter Sunday breakfast.

Ingredients:

1 large cake of yeast or 3 packages dry
    rapid rise yeast
4 cups whole milk
16 cups flour (15 cups if using dry
    rapid rise yeast)
6 large eggs (5 extra large)
2 sticks butter
2 cups granulated sugar
1 teaspoon salt

Directions:

    Put milk into a sauce pot and scald, then let cool to warm (about 100 – to 110 degrees), then add yeast. Melt the butter and let cool. Beat the eggs and gradually beat in the sugar. Add yeast mixture to the eggs and then add the cooled butter. Place all the wet ingredients in a large bowl, large enough to hold the flour. Gradually, add the flour about one cup at a time until all the flour has been incorporated. After the dough is well mixed, you can transfer it onto a floured board to knead for 10-15 minutes until the dough becomes elastic and bubbly. If the quantity of dough is too large to handle, divide it into two amounts to knead. After kneading the dough, form it into one large ball, then

put the ball into a large buttered bowl. Cover the bowl with plastic wrap and a clean cloth, and let it rise till doubled for about 45-60 minutes.

    This dough will make 3-4 *paska* breads, depending on the amount of dough you use for decorating each loaf. (I usually make one larger bread for my basket and two smaller ones because I like to elaborately decorate my breads.) Put each bread into a buttered baking pan, brush with egg wash, and let rise for 45 minutes. Bake at 350 degrees for 30-45 minutes. This depends on the size of your bread. If your bread is getting too brown, cover it with foil. Let bread cool for about 10 minutes before removing from the pan.

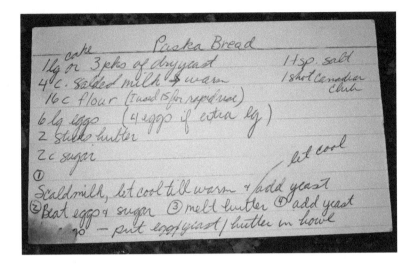

Horseradish with Beets *Cwikla*

Ingredients:

3 cups cooked beets
6 ounces prepared horseradish
1 teaspoon white vinegar
¼ teaspoon salt
1 tablespoon brown sugar

Directions:

Drain the beets very well and finely chop them. A food processor can be used to chop them. Add the other ingredients and blend by hand. Refrigerate. (Best if made a few days in advance, the ingredients are able to mingle.)

Mom's Stuffed Cabbage Rolls *Golabki (literally means pigeons in Polish) or Halupki*

A classic Polish meal that was often served for Sunday dinner in our home was stuffed cabbage rolls. This Polish delicacy can be traced to a Polish myth as early as the mid 1400's when King Casimir IV fed his army *golabki* before an important battle of the Thirteen Years War (1454-1466). The army attributed their victory to this hearty meat and rice dish that gave them strength and endurance.

In a family of great cooks, everyone thought my mother's *halupki* were the best. What made her *halupki* different was not only the good ingredients she used but the way she rolled her cabbage, uniquely tucking in the filled cabbage roll on each side of the roll. This technique is shown in the picture.

For the best cabbage rolls, it is important to have the right cabbage leaves. Look for large heads with the most outer dark green leaves or ask your produce manager to save the outer leaves when the cabbage is trimmed. This recipe makes about 15 rolls, depending on the size of the cabbage leaves.

Ingredients:

2 heads cabbage with leafy outer leaves
1 large onion chopped
4 green onions chopped with most of the
   green part
½ cup chopped parsley
1 pound ground chuck beef
1 pound ground veal (beef or pork can be
   substituted)
1 pound ground pork
1 to 1½ cups uncooked rice (depending if
   you like more rice)
Salt and pepper to taste
3 cans tomato condensed soup
Water

Directions:

Remove the outer leaves from the cabbage. Core each head of cabbage. This allows you to take off the steamed leaves easier. Place the entire heads and outer leaves in a large pot of boiling water and let steam until the leaves become soft and pliable enough to remove. Remove as many of the outer leaves that can be taken from both heads of the steaming cabbage.

Be careful not to tear or damage the steamed leaves. Place the leaves on a large baking sheet to cool. Also take the remaining heads of cabbage out of the pot. (This cabbage will be chopped and placed in the bottom of your cooking pot to help prevent your rolls from burning and gives your sauce more flavor.).

The next step is to make the meat filling. Into a large bowl, add the meats, rice, onion, parsley, ½ can of tomato soup, and salt and pepper. Mix all the ingredients well and set aside.

Prior to stuffing the cabbage, cut the hard core center stems and veins from the cabbage leaves. (This enables the cabbage to be rolled easier.) Depending on the size of the cabbage leaf, fill the center of each leaf with about ½ cup or more of filling. Starting at the stem end, begin to enclose

the meat filling tightly. Tuck in each end of the leaf by pushing in gently with your index finger. Place each roll seam side down. Repeat until all of the filling is used.

To cook the rolls, first roughly chop the remaining cabbage and put on the bottom of the pot. Place the cabbage rolls on the chopped cabbage. Top with the remaining 2½ cans of tomato soup, 2-3 cans of water, and salt and pepper. Cover and bring to a boil. Reduce heat and simmer for about 1-2 hours depending on the size of your cabbage rolls. Serve hot.

Beet Pickled Eggs

I have fond memories of my grandmother's homemade canned beets lined in rows on a shelf in her basement, always saving a few jars for this Easter recipe. Since most of us do not grow our own beets or can them, the following recipe is made with canned beets from the grocery store.

Ingredients:

1 dozen extra large hard boiled eggs, peeled
2 cans sliced or cubed beets and the juice
1 medium onion, sliced in half moons
1 cup white vinegar
1 teaspoon salt

Directions:

In a 2-3 quart container, place one can of beets, half of the onions and the cooked eggs. Add the remaining ingredients. Cover and refrigerate. It is best to make at least 3-4 days before serving so that the whites of the eggs have enough time to turn beautiful beet red!

Mickey's Easter Cottage Cheese *Kolache/Kolaczki*

Ingredients for Step 1:

3 pounds creamed cottage cheese

3 egg yolks

2-8 ounce packages Philadelphia Cream
   Cheese

2 cups sugar

8-10 tablespoon Tapioca

2 teaspoon vanilla

Zest of 2 lemons

Directions for Step 1:

Mix all of the ingredients well and let rest for
2 hours.

Ingredients for Step 2:

2 cups lukewarm whole milk

¾ cup sugar

¾ cake of household yeast or 2½ packages of
   dry yeast

2 cups flour

Directions for Step 2:

Mix all of the ingredients well and let rise for
45 minutes.

Ingredients for Step 3:

6 cups flour

2 teaspoons salt

1½ cups butter

4 eggs

Directions for Step 3:

Mix the first three ingredients together to make the
dough, as if you are making a pie crust. Add the eggs
to the mixture and blend well. Then add the yeast
sponge mixture from Step 2 to this mixture. Mix well.
Let stand 15 minutes.

*Please note: This photograph was taken using cherry filling
rather than the cheese filling to enhance the criss-cross design
process.*

Divide the dough into 8 balls. Each ball will make
one roll. Roll each ball into a rectangle shape. Put about
⅛ of the cheese filling down the middle of the rolled
rectangle. As shown in the picture, cut approximately
11 even strips on each side of the filling. Beginning
at the top of the roll, take the first strip of dough and
cross it over the filling, making sure that the end is
tucked and pinched under the roll. Then on the
opposite side of the roll, take the first strip and cross it

over remembering to tuck and pinch it under the roll. Keep repeating this process in a criss-crossed design until all the strips have been crossed. The roll should be tight so the filling does not come out. Transfer roll to a greased baking sheet and let rise for about 30-45 minutes. Bake at 350 degrees for 30-35 minutes. This recipe makes 8 rolls. They freeze well.

Vegetables *Polonaise Jarzyny po Polsku*

"*A la Polonaise,*" which means "in the Polish style," is a unique and distinctly Polish way of seasoning any hot vegetable. The buttery-toasted bread crumbs add a delicious and unexpected crunch to any steamed or boiled vegetable. A *la Polonaise* is especially good with cauliflower, asparagus, potatoes or carrots.

Ingredients:

6 tablespoons butter
1 cup plain white bread crumbs
Zest of 1 lemon
½ teaspoon paprika
1 tablespoons fresh dill, chopped
Salt and pepper to taste

Directions:

First, toast the bread crumbs in a dry skillet over medium heat for about a minute. Remove and transfer into a bowl and set aside. Heat butter in a skillet and let come to a slight boil for about a minute. Add bread crumbs and paprika and brown until crisp and golden. Remove from the heat to avoid further browning. Sprinkle bread crumbs, lemon zest and dill on top of the hot and lightly buttered and seasoned cooked vegetables. (Optional: garnish with a chopped hard-boiled egg)

Noodles, *Pieroghi, Haluski, Pagach,* and More

Polish Dumplings *Haluski*

Cottage Cheese and Noodle Casserole

Polish Style Cabbage and Noodles *Kluski z Kapusta po Polski*

Fruit *Pieroghi*

Blueberry *Pieroghi*

Plum *Pieroghi*

Plum Dumplings

Pagach

Polish Dumplings *Haluski*

I have included two basic *haluski* recipes. Traditionally, *haluski* are served with fried cabbage or in soups and stews, but really the possibilities are quite endless.

Recipe #1 is best served with fried cabbage or sautéed sauerkraut or in soups and stews, while recipe #2 is more flavorful as a great starch with any meal; just season with butter.

My grandmother told me that in her day, a woman's cooking skills were judged by the size of her *haluski*—the smaller, which are more difficult to make, the better.

Haluski Recipe #1

Ingredients:

2 cups all purpose flour

4 eggs, slightly beaten

¼ cup water

1 teaspoon salt

Or

Haluski Recipe #2

Ingredients:

2 eggs, slightly beaten

¼ cup water

1 to 1½ cups flour

1 teaspoon baking powder

½ teaspoon seasoned salt

1 teaspoon paprika, dried dill or marjoram

Directions:

Put a large pot of salted water on the stove and let come to a fast simmer. Meanwhile, add eggs and water in a large bowl and beat well. Then, a little at a time, add all of the dry ingredients and mix well. The dough should be soft and sticky. Put about a cup of the dough on the edge of a flat dinner plate. With a spoon, cut off a very small amount of the dough and let drop into the simmering water (this will form small unformed dumplings). Dipping your spoon

into the boiling water will help to make the dough slide off the plate easier. When the dumplings are cooked, they will rise to the top of the water, about 2-3 minutes. Remove the *haluski* with a slotted spoon and put into a strainer with a bowl underneath to collect the water. Repeat this process until all the dough is used.

Depending on the use of the dumplings, you may want to return them to a bowl and add 6 tablespoon melted butter and salt and pepper to taste. (The only way that I would not add the butter to the cooked *haluski* is if the dumplings will be served in soup.)

Cottage Cheese and Noodle Casserole

Ingredients:

1 pound noodles (medium cut)
1 pound creamed cottage cheese
4 eggs
½ cup of granulated sugar
6 ounces butter
Salt and pepper to taste
¼ teaspoon nutmeg (optional)
1 teaspoon cinnamon (optional)

Directions:

Boil noodles according to directions on the package. Drain noodles and put them in a large bowl. Beat eggs well and add sugar, 4 ounce melted butter, salt and pepper and optional spices. Add cottage cheese to the noodles and egg mixture. Mix all of the ingredients well and put into a buttered 9" x 11" baking pan. Cut the remaining butter on the top and bake at 350 degrees for about 30-45 minutes until the top is brown and bubbly.

Polish Style Cabbage and Noodles *Kluski z Kapusta po Polski*

Ingredients:

1 large head of cabbage (8 cups), coarsely chopped in 1½ inch pieces
1 large onion, chopped
1 teaspoon caraway seed (optional)
3 tablespoons vegetable oil or more
4 tablespoons butter
1 pound wide egg noodles
Salt and pepper to taste

Directions:

Heat the oil and butter in a large pot or Dutch oven and add cabbage, onion and salt and pepper. Sauté on medium high heat for about 25 minutes until cabbage is tender. You may need to add more oil to the cabbage. While the cabbage is cooking, boil noodles according to the directions on the package or el dente. When cabbage is cooked and tender, add the noodles and butter to the cabbage (you may not want to add all of the noodles, if you prefer more cabbage and less noodles). Add caraway seeds, and additional salt and pepper to taste. Serve with a side of cottage cheese.

Fruit *Pieroghi*

Included in the Christmas section of this book you will find the recipe for classic savory *pieroghi* with three yummy fillings: potato and cheese, sauerkraut, and prune. Below I have included my favorite sweet "dessert" *pieroghi* recipes using blueberries and plums, although you can use numerous summer fruit varieties. Don't let the summer pass without making a batch or two of these that are the ultimate summer treat! After they are boiled, I like to garnish with melted butter, sweetened sour cream, and a pinch of sugar.

Blueberry *Pieroghi*

Fresh blueberry *pieroghi* are simply delicious and the filling could not be easier.

To make these *pieroghi* you will find the recipe for basic *pieroghi* dough on page 8.

Ingredients:
4 cups fresh blueberries
2 tablespoons flour
1 tablespoon powdered sugar

Lily and PJ pick blueberries for their *pieroghi*.

Directions for preparing the blueberries:

Wash fresh berries and let dry on paper towel. Mix flour and powdered sugar together. Put dry berries in a bowl and sprinkle with the flour mixture to lightly coat the berries. To fill the *pieroghi*, place a heaping tablespoon of berries in the center of your circular dough, then fold dough over and close the *pieroghi* by crimping the edges together.

Plum *Pieroghi*

This fresh fruit *pieroghi* is considered a dessert by many and is simply delicious. I like to make them in September, when the small Italian plums are in season.

To make these *pieroghi* you will find the recipe for basic *pieroghi* dough on page 8.

Ingredients:

24 small ripe Italian plums

24-½ teaspoon sugar cubes or ½ teaspoon of loose granulated sugar

Directions for preparing the plums:

Starting at the stem end of the plum, make a slit carefully not to cut the plum entirely in half, and remove the pit. In the cavity created by removing the pit, stuff the plum with a sugar cube, close it and slightly push it down. Each plum will make one *pieroghi*. Place plum in the center of your circular dough, then fold dough over and close the *pieroghi* by crimping the edges together.

Cooking the *Pieroghi*:

Add each *pieroghi* individually to a large pot of boiling water that has been salted. Don't overload the pot! Let the *pieroghi* boil for about 5-6 minutes and when they float to the top they are ready to take out of the water. Carefully remove them with a slotted spoon or wire basket-type utensil and place in a shallow serving bowl or plate. Drizzle with melted butter and sprinkle with granulated sugar and a hearty dollop of sweetened sour cream "Polish cream."

Ingredients for Sweetened Sour Cream:

2 cups sour cream

1 cup sugar

1 teaspoon nutmeg (optional)

Directions:

Add one pint of sour cream to a bowl and stir in one cup of sugar. Mix well. It will take a few minutes for the sugar to dissolve. Add nutmeg and refrigerate until ready to serve.

Plum Dumplings

These dumplings are wonderful as a dessert, side dish, or a meal. Unfortunately, you can only make them in September when the plums are in season and available in the grocery stores. In Eastern Europe, each country has its own version. The dough in this recipe is made with potatoes and I've given you two choices on how to serve them: (option #1) with bread crumbs, cinnamon and sugar, or (option #2) with dry cottage cheese, butter, sugar and cinnamon. The latter is my family's favorite!

Ingredients:

5 pounds potatoes that have been peeled, boiled and mashed
2 eggs, slightly beaten
2 - 2½ cups flour
1 tablespoon melted butter, cooled
18-20 Italian prune plums, pitted
18-20 sugar cubes
8 teaspoons butter
¼ cup sugar
2 teaspoons cinnamon
1½ cups very fine white bread crumbs (Option #1)
2 cups large curd dry cottage cheese (Option #2)

Directions:

Wash and pit the plums and set aside. In a bowl, combine the cooled potatoes, eggs, butter and salt. Then add the flour, a little at a time to form a soft dough that is easy to work with (you may need to add a little more flour). Divide the dough into three balls, cover with your bowl and let rest for about 30 minutes. Place a sugar cube in the center of each pitted plum and close the plum. Then on a lightly floured board, working with one ball of dough, roll the dough to about ¼ inch thickness and cut into three inch squares. Place a plum in the center of the dough and completely cover the plum with dough, pinching all of the seams together to seal, pressing out all of the air. Moisten the edges with water if you are having trouble crimping the dough together. Repeat this process until you have used all of the dough.

Gently place the dumplings into the boiling water, a few at a time. Cook for about 25 minutes. Remove dumplings from the pot, a few at a time, and let them drain.

Option One

Melt 8 teaspoons of butter in a skillet over medium heat. Stir in the bread crumbs and the sugar and cook until lightly brown. Transfer the breadcrumb mixture to a shallow pan and roll warm dumplings to coat in the mixture. Add additional sugar and butter if desired.

Option Two

Put melted butter into a shallow baking dish. Place the cooked dumplings into the pan with butter, mix well to coat the dumplings with butter, add cottage cheese, and sprinkle with the cinnamon-sugar mixture. Heat your oven to 350 degrees, bake for 15 minutes, then serve.

Pagach

Pagach is wonderful yeast bread that is rolled thin and traditionally stuffed with a potato or cabbage filling. This Eastern European dish is somewhat universal and has many variations, depending on the country of origin. My grandmother often made it when she baked bread and I have prioritized this as one of my favorite childhood comfort foods. *Pagach* is a vegetarian entrée or a hearty accompaniment to soup or a salad. The dough can be rolled into a circle, like a pizza, or in a rectangular shape. The fillings may also vary according to your preferences. I use the same potato filling that I make for pieroghi.

Note: *Frozen bread or fresh pizza dough also works well with this recipe.*

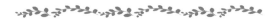

Ingredients for Dough:

2½ -3 cups all-purpose flour
½ teaspoon salt
1 cup warm water
1 package dry active rising yeast
Sea salt and coarsely ground black pepper
   (optional)

Directions for Dough:

Dissolve the yeast in the warm water (about 105 degrees). Place the flour and salt in a bowl and gradually stir in the liquid. After mixed, put dough on lightly floured surface and knead for about 7-10 minutes. If the dough is too sticky, add a little flour. When dough is smooth and elastic, form into a ball and place in a greased bowl and cover. Let rise until about double in size.

Next punch down the dough and place on lightly floured surface and divide into 2 balls. Cover and let rest for 15 minutes. Roll one ball into a rectangle shape about 9 x 12 inches or a 12 inch circle. (Tip: For easy pickup of your *pagach*, place bottom rolled dough on a greased sheet of parchment paper.) Next, add the filling, leaving about a 1 inch border. Roll your second piece of dough to match the same size as your first piece and place it on top of the filling. Seal the edges carefully by pinching or crimping like you would a pie. Make a few vent holes to allow the steam to escape, like a pie. You can do this with a fork or the point of a sharp knife. Brush the entire *pagach* with melted butter or oil and then sprinkle with sea salt and coarsely ground black pepper (optional). Carefully lift the entire piece of parchment paper with the *pagach* on it to a large baking sheet, cover with plastic wrap and let rise for about 20-30 minutes. Place baking sheet into a preheated 375-degree oven. Bake for about 30 minutes. Cool on a rack.

Potato Filling Ingredients:

5-6 Large Russet potatoes, peeled, cubed and
    boiled till tender
8 ounces of shredded Colby Longhorn cheese
Salt and pepper to taste
1 medium onion, chopped and sautéed in
3 tablespoons butter (optional)

Directions:

Cook potatoes and drain. While hot, mash
cooked potatoes add cheese, onions (optional)
and salt and pepper. Let cool before filling the
pagach.

Cabbage Filling Ingredients:

1 head of cabbage cored and chopped
1 large onion chopped
Salt and Pepper to taste
½ cup oil

Directions:

Place all of the ingredients in a pot or Dutch oven
and saute until tender. Let cool before filling the
pagach.

Soups *Zupa*

The heart of polish cuisine is *zupa*. The repertoire of soup recipes in this book are simple to make, take about an hour of cooking time, and are very economical. Also, many are vegetarian. Every recipe I love, and I think you will too!

Beet Barszcz *Czysty Czerwony*

Polish Potato Soup *Zupa Kartoflana* with Polish Meatball (optional)

Great-grandma Rose's Cabbage Soup with Ham

Mom's Classic Chicken Soup

Slovak Style Hearty Bean and Ham Soup

Cream of *Kohlrabi* Soup

Grandma Mary's Green Bean and *Zapraska* Soup

Polish Stew *Gulasz Wieprzowy*

Beet Barszcz *Czysty Czerwony*

This recipe sautés the beets which really intensifies the flavor. To make a delicious vegetarian soup, simply substitute vegetable broth for the beef broth.

Ingredients:

4 large beets (about 5 cups) peeled and cut into 1-inch cubes
2 large onions, chopped
½ head or about 3 cups cabbage thinly sliced
3 carrots, scraped and cubed
1 large russet potatoes (about 1 cup) peeled and cut in 1-inch cubes
3 tablespoons flat leaf parsley, chopped
8 cups beef stock
3 tablespoons red wine or cider vinegar
1 teaspoon sugar
2 tablespoons olive oil
1 cup sour cream
1 tablespoon fresh dill, chopped (optional)
Salt and pepper to taste

Directions:

In a large stock pot, add oil and beets and cook over medium heat for about 3 minutes. Then add onions, carrots, salt, pepper and sugar and continue to sauté the mixture for about 5 minutes. Add beef stock and the remaining ingredients (except vinegar and sour cream). Bring to a boil and let simmer for about an hour until the vegetables are very tender. Taste the soup and add more seasoning if necessary.

Stir in the vinegar. Serve immediately while hot. Garnish with a dollop of sour cream and a little fresh dill. Homemade *haluski* go well with this soup. (The recipe may be found in this book on page 35.)

Polish Potato Soup *Zupa Kartoflana* with Polish Meatball (optional)

For real "meat and potato" lovers, these meatballs are a hearty addition to this soup, but the soup is delicious and can stand alone without them.

Ingredients for Soup:

3 pounds potatoes (7-8 large potatoes peeled and cut into 1½-inch cubes)
3-4 carrots, scraped and sliced
1 large onion, coarsely chopped
3 stalks celery, chopped
2 cups chicken broth
1 cup sour cream
2 tablespoons flour
1 tablespoon fresh dill, chopped
Salt and pepper to taste

Directions for Soup:

In a large stock pot place all of the vegetables and cover with chicken broth and enough water to barely cover the vegetables, about 1½ cups, and add salt and pepper. Cook vegetables until tender about 30 minutes.

Cream together the sour cream and flour and then temper the mixture by adding 1 cup of the hot soup liquid into the sour cream and stir. Then add the sour cream mixture to the soup and the cooked meatballs (optional) and let simmer for 5-10 minutes. Serve

soup with 2-3 meatballs per serving and garnish with fresh dill and coarsely ground pepper.

Ingredients for Meatballs:

2 tablespoons of vegetable oil
1 pound ground chuck
1 pound ground pork
1 egg
½ cup milk
3 large slices stale bread
2 large onions, chopped
1 teaspoon sugar
1 teaspoon paprika
2 tablespoons of each: parsley and marjoram
Salt and pepper to taste
1 cup flour to coat the meatballs seasoned with salt and pepper and paprika
3 tablespoons of each for frying meatballs: butter and vegetable oil

Directions for meatballs:

First sauté the onions that will be incorporated into the meatballs. In a medium skillet add oil, onions, paprika and salt and pepper. To get a good caramelization add sugar to the onions and sauté for about 5-7 minutes. Remove onions from heat and let cool. To make the meatball filling combine meat, eggs, bread (that has been soaked in milk and the excess milk has been squeezed out), dill, parsley, paprika, cooked onions and salt and pepper. Mix well and form the mixture into small balls, about 1 inch in diameter. Season the four with salt and pepper and paprika, then lightly roll the meat balls in the seasoned flour.

In a large skillet melt 3 tablespoons of butter and 2 tablespoons of oil together over medium high heat. Add meat balls, a small batch at a time, and fry until lightly browned on all sides about 5-7 minutes. You may need to add more butter and oil. Remove each batch of meatballs to a shallow dish that has been lined with paper towel to absorb the excess fat. Then add the meatballs to the soup and let simmer in the soup for 5-10 minutes.

Great-Grandma Rose's Cabbage Soup with Ham

This peasant soup recipe was brought from Poland and was my great-grandmother's favorite. It has only three ingredients but is so flavorful.

Ingredients:

1 large head of green cabbage, cored and
    chopped into large pieces (I choose
    cabbage with dark green outer leaves)
3 cups ham, chopped in large 1 inch cubes
    (if you have a ham bone, add this also,
    it will make the soup even richer and
    more flavorful)
4 large russet potatoes, peeled and quartered
Salt and pepper to taste

Directions:

Put all of the ingredients in a soup pot, cover with water and let soup come to a boil and simmer for at least one hour until the cabbage is very tender. You cannot believe how delicious! Serve piping hot.

Mom's Classic Chicken Soup

This recipe calls for a lot of vegetables, but you may use less, of course.

Ingredients:

1 whole chicken about 3-4 pounds
4 cups carrots, scraped and sliced into thick
    rounds
4 cups celery, chopped
½ cup parsley, chopped
4 cups onion, chopped
3 pear shaped tomatoes from a can without
    liquid, squeeze by hand
4 cups fresh greens (endive, escarole or
    spinach), chopped
Salt and pepper to taste
5 Maggi chicken bouillon cubes

Directions:

In a large stock pot, place chicken and barely cover with water (it depends on the size of the pot and if you like more broth, about 2-3 quarts of water). Over medium heat bring soup to a boil and gently boil for about 40 minutes. Skim the frothy matter from the soup with a large spoon and discard. Add all of the ingredients except greens and let simmer for about 1½ hours. Remove the cooked chicken from the pot and place in a shallow pan to cool. Add greens and let simmer for about 20 minutes until tender. When cool enough to work with, remove skin and bones from the chicken and then discard. Break or cut the chicken into large bite size pieces, then add chicken and all of its juice back into the pot. Serve soup piping hot. Homemade noodles or *haluski* go well with this soup. (The recipe may be found in this book on page 35.)

Slovak Style Hearty Bean and Ham Soup

Ingredients:

1 pound dried great northern beans
6 cups water
4 cups chicken broth
2 cups onions, chopped
2 cups celery, chopped
2 cups carrots, scraped and chopped
2 cloves garlic, minced
1 ham bone
2-3 cups ham, cubed
2-3 tablespoons tomato paste
½ teaspoon of crushed red pepper flakes
2 tablespoons olive oil
3 tablespoons chopped parsley
Salt and pepper to taste

Directions:

The night before you make the soup add beans to a large pot and cover with water. Bring to a rapid boil, cover, remove from the heat and let soak overnight. In the morning, prior to making the soup, drain and rinse the beans in a colander.

In a large stock pot add oil, garlic, ham bone and red pepper flakes and sauté for three minutes. Add beans, water, tomato paste, ham and broth. Bring to a boil and let simmer for about 45 minutes. At this point taste your soup, season and add celery, carrots, onions and parsley. Let cook for about an hour until the beans and vegetables are tender. If you like your soup thinner, you may want to add more water or broth. Remove bone from soup and take off the meat, putting the ham and its juices back in the soup.

Cream of *Kohlrabi* Soup

Kohlrabi is a very popular vegetable among Eastern Europeans. My grandmother grew kohlrabi in her garden and I have fond memories of eating them raw with a little salt and also savoring them in this creamy pale green soup.

Ingredients:

1 large onion, chopped
2 stalks of celery, chopped
2 carrots, scraped and chopped
4 large kohlrabi, peeled and cubed (about 4-5 cups)
2 large potatoes, peeled and cubed
4-5 cups chicken broth
4-5 tablespoons butter
2 tablespoons flour
3 tablespoons parsley, chopped
⅓ cup half and half
Salt and pepper to taste (white pepper is optional)
Dash of nutmeg

Directions:

In a stock pot, heat 2-3 tablespoons of butter and add the onions. Sauté the onions for about three minutes until they become translucent. Add the other vegetables, chicken broth, seasonings and parsley. Bring to a boil, then reduce heat and simmer for about 45 minutes or until the vegetables are very tender. Make a *zapraska* (Polish roux) to thicken the soup by melting 2 tablespoons of butter in a small sauce pan and then adding the flour. Cook the flour mixture stirring constantly for about two minutes. Add about one or two cups of the hot soup into the flour mixture along with the half and half, and stir to blend well. Add this mixture back into the soup, stir well to blend and simmer for about 15 more minutes. Serve hot. (This soup freezes well.)

Grandma Mary's Green Bean and *Zapraska* Soup

This peasant soup recipe was brought from Poland and was my grandmother's favorite. She made it when the fresh green beans from her garden were at their peak. This is a family favorite.

Ingredients:

3 pounds green beans, ends trimmed
6 red potatoes, cubed
2 large onions, chopped
1 pound sliced bacon, cut into ½ inch pieces
2 cups ham, cubed (optional)
6 tablespoons flour
3 tablespoons parsley
3 Maggi beef bouillon cubes
Salt and pepper to taste

Directions:

In a large stock pot, place beans and add water to about an inch below bean level (about 8 cups). Also, add ham, parsley, salt, pepper and Maggi seasoning. When beans come to a boil, add potatoes. Simmer until the vegetables are tender.

While the beans are simmering, cook bacon in a large skillet for about 5 minutes and then add onions. Cook over medium heat until the bacon gets very crisp and the onions get golden brown. This will give your soup a rich color and flavor. Next, make a *zapraska* (a Polish roux) that will thicken the soup. Stir the flour into the bacon mixture, add salt and pepper to the mixture and cook flour for about two minutes, stirring constantly. Temper your *zapraska* by adding about 2 cups of the hot liquid from the beans into the bacon–flour mixture, stirring constantly until well blended, then remove from heat and set aside. This bacon-flour *zapraska* will thicken and flavor the soup. When the green beans and potatoes are tender, add the bacon-flour mixture to the green beans stirring well to distribute the mixture. Let the soup come to a boil and simmer for about 5 more minutes. Serve hot and enjoy.

Polish Stew *Gulasz Wieprzowy*

As the Irish have their stew made with lamb, the Poles have their stew made with pork, since it is the most popular meat in Poland. The uniqueness of this recipe is the pork, rather than beef, which gives the dish a very Polish flavor.

Ingredients:

2 pounds pork shoulder, cubed
2 large onions, chopped
4 carrots, diced
2 stalks celery, chopped
1 turnip, peeled and diced
2 tablespoons tomato paste
½ cup beer
4 cups water or beef stock
3 tablespoons oil
1 cup flour
1 teaspoon paprika
¼ teaspoon caraway seeds
¼ teaspoon marjoram
Salt and pepper to taste

Directions:

Season flour with salt and pepper and ½ teaspoon paprika and lightly dredge meat in flour (reserve a heaping tablespoon of the flour for later). In a Dutch oven or stockpot, heat oil to medium high and add meat, browning on all sides. Remove meat from pot, reduce heat to medium, add onions and sauté for 3 minutes until translucent. Return meat and all of its juice, carrots, celery, turnip, beer, stock and spices to pot. Cover pot and let the stew simmer for about 1 to 1½ hours until meat is tender. Add the reserved 1 tablespoon of flour to sour cream and mix well. Add sour cream to the stew and let simmer for about 5 minutes. Serve hot with *haluski* (optional). (The recipe may be found in this book on page 35.)

The Main Course

Fresh Salmon Salad Romanov

Easy *Kielbasa Kulebiak*

Esterhazy Steak

Aunt Doris's Chicken *Paprikash Csirke Paprikas*

Kolet Schabowy Breaded Pork Tenderloin: "My Way"

Horseradish Crusted Salmon with Dill Sauce

Black Mountain Pork Chops

Rusyn Beef Roulades

Kielbasa Stewed with Tomatoes and Vegetables

Kulebiak

Fresh Salmon Salad Romanov

This is an easy and delicious cold salad fit for any special occasion. Guaranteed to please even a Romanov.

Ingredients:

1 pound of cooked salmon (remove skin and breakup into large pieces)
1 cup celery, chopped
1 cup frozen peas, defrosted
2 tablespoons shallots, minced
1 tablespoon fresh dill
2 tablespoons fresh lemon juice
1 cup mayonnaise
Salt and pepper to taste

Directions:

Place all of the ingredients in a bowl. Mix well to distribute the mayonnaise, trying not to break up the salmon. Chill for one hour and serve.

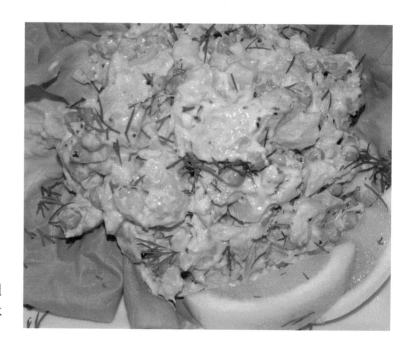

Easy *Kielbasa Kulebiak*

Ingredients:

1 pound of good quality kielbasa (cut into four equal parts)
1 package of refrigerated French bread dough
1 egg for egg wash

Directions:

Preheat oven to 350 degrees. Lightly grease baking sheet and set aside.

Unroll the package of crusty French bread and using a rolling pin, roll the dough to a rectangle shape about 13 inches by 11 inches. Cut the dough into 4 equal rectangles. Place the each piece of kielbasa on a piece of dough and fold the dough over the kielbasa. Seal the edges very carefully. Place each *kulebiak* seam side down on the baking sheet. Brush with egg wash and bake for about 25 minutes until golden brown.

(Optional: Slightly butterfly the kielbasa and top with cooked sauerkraut. Wrap in dough following the directions.)

Esterhazy Steak

For those of you who are wondering what is "Esterhazy," let me explain. Esterhazy was an aristocratic Magyar family in the Kingdom of Hungary. In the 18th century, they were the largest landowners in the Hapsburg Empire. Their income exceeded that of the Hapsburg Emperor. Most of their lands were located in present day Austria, Slovakia, and Hungary. The Esterhazy name has been attached to numerous culinary delights including the following recipe. This recipe is quick and simple, but also quite elegant and delicious.

Ingredients:

2-3 tablespoons olive oil
4 filet mignon steaks about 6-8 ounces each
  and cut about ½ to 1 inch thick
2 carrots, cut into matchsticks
2 shallots, minced
2 parsnips, cut into matchsticks
1 teaspoon sweet paprika
1 cup sour cream
1 tablespoon butter
⅓ cup vodka
Salt and pepper to taste

Directions:

Remove steaks from the refrigerator, about 30 minutes before cooking. Pat steaks dry with paper towel and season with salt and pepper. In a medium sized skillet, heat oil until hot, add steaks and sear on each side for about 3-4 minutes on each side on medium high heat. (The time depends on the thickness of the steak and how you prefer your meat.) Remove the steaks from the pan, put on a plate, loosely covered with foil. Reduce the heat to medium, add butter, the vegetables, and sauté for about 2 minutes until they are al dente. Add salt, pepper and the paprika to the vegetables. To make the sauce, add vodka, then stir in the sour cream and let the sauce warm but not boil. Return the steaks and their juices back in the pan to warm for about two minutes. Serve immediately. Best accompaniments are buttered *haluski*, noodles or *spatzel*.

Aunt Doris's Chicken *Paprikash Csirke Paprikas*

What a fond memory… my aunt lovingly made this dish for me when I went to visit her in Ohio. She served the wonderful chicken on a bed of homemade buttered *haluski*.

Ingredients:

3 tablespoons oil
3-4 pounds chicken with skin and bones (I like to use only chicken breasts)
½ cup flour
3 teaspoons sweet paprika
2 medium-large onions, chopped
4 cloves garlic, chopped
2 cups chicken broth
2 8-ounce cans of tomato sauce
1 tablespoon sugar
2 cups sour cream
Salt and pepper to taste
2 tablespoons parsley, chopped (for garnish)

Noodles

Ingredients:

1 pound of wide egg noodles, cooked
1 tablespoon fresh dill, chopped
2 tablespoons fresh parsley, chopped
4 tablespoons butter

Directions:

In a shallow pan, mix flour with salt, pepper, and 1 teaspoon paprika. Lightly coat the chicken in the flour mixture. In a large Dutch oven heat the oil using medium heat. Add chicken skin side down, and brown on both sides for about 12-15 minutes. Chicken will not be completely cooked at this point but remove from the Dutch oven. Add onions and garlic and sauté for about 4 minutes. You may need to add a little more oil at this point. Then add the tomato sauce, sugar, 2 teaspoons paprika, salt and

pepper, and chicken broth. Blend all the liquid well, and place the chicken back into the Dutch oven. Put the lid on the Dutch oven, reduce the heat and let simmer for about 45 minutes (The time varies according to the size of the chicken pieces. The chicken should be very tender but not falling apart.) Remove the chicken to a serving platter. Add the sour cream to the liquid mixture in the Dutch oven and blend well. Heat until just hot, do not let boil. Taste, you may need to re-season at this point. On a large serving platter, place noodles that have been buttered and seasoned with salt and pepper, dill and parsley, top with chicken and then spoon sour cream sauce over chicken. Garnish with chopped fresh parsley.

Note: I like to serve this dish the old fashioned way with haluski. (The recipe may be found in this book on page 35.)

Kolet Schabowy Breaded Pork Tenderloin: "My Way"

This is an updated version of the classic breaded pork chops that has less fat, fewer calories and takes less time to prepare. But most of all, it is a winner. Everyone loves it!

Ingredients:

1 whole pork tenderloin about 24 ounces
  (I prefer the type that has been pre-
  marinated. My favorite marinade for this
  recipe is garlic and lemon.)
1 cup seasoned bread crumbs
Salt and pepper to taste
¼ cup olive oil

Directions:

Note: For easy cleanup: put bread crumbs on a large piece of waxed paper to roll the tenderloin.

Remove tenderloin from the plastic wrap and roll meat onto the bread crumbs, pressing and covering pork completely. Put oil in the bottom of a small shallow baking dish and place tenderloin that has been breaded. Bake in a preheated 400-degree oven for 30 minutes. Take out the roast, using tongs, gently turn the meat completely over so the bottom is on the top. Drizzle a little more oil and continue baking for another 30-35 minutes. Remove from oven and let rest for 10 minutes before slicing.

Horseradish Crusted Salmon with Dill Sauce

Ingredients:

1½ pounds salmon with skin removed,
   cut into five 2-inch pieces or form into
   medallions as in the picture
½ cup freshly grated horseradish
½ cup grated Granny Smith apple
2 egg whites, slightly beaten
¼ cup parsley
2 tablespoons freshly squeezed lemon juice
Salt and pepper
2 tablespoons melted butter for frying

Directions:

   To the freshly grated horseradish and apple, add remaining ingredients and blend well. The mixture will make a thick paste. Set the paste aside while cutting the salmon and seasoning both sides. Carefully place about a tablespoon of paste on the top of each salmon piece.

   Brush the saute pan with the melted butter, then heat the pan to medium high heat before adding the salmon, horseradish side down. Cook until the horseradish forms a golden crust, about 2-3 minutes. Lower the heat to medium and cook the bottom side of the salmon about 2 minutes or until done to your preference.

   Note: to form a salmon medallion, cut two ¾ inch strips of salmon, form into circular shape, and tie each circle with butcher string. Cook with string and remove before serving.

Ingredients for Dill Sauce:

4 teaspoons butter
¼ cup flour
2 tablespoons fresh dill, chopped
2 tablespoons fresh lemon juice
1 cup sour cream
½ cup hot water
Salt and pepper to taste

Directions for Dill Sauce:

   For the dill sauce, make a *zapraska* by melting butter into a small saucepan and whisking in the flour. Cook for about 2 minutes, then add the remaining ingredients. Bring to a boil and serve immediately.

Black Mountain Pork Chops

In the 1950s, mystery author Rex Stout created a larger than life fictional detective, Nero Wolfe, who had a love affair with great food. In his book, *The Black Mountain,* Wolfe immortalized this Yugoslavian specialty. The book is set in Montenegro, which literally means "Black Mountain." These chops are delicious any time of the year, especially in the fall. I'm sure you will agree with "foodie," Nero Wolf!

Ingredients:

4 (eight ounce) center cut pork chops
3 tablespoons oil
3 cloves garlic, minced
2 cups onions, finely chopped
2-3 tart apples, peeled and thinly sliced
¼ cup flour
¼ teaspoon paprika
Salt and pepper to taste

Sauce Ingredients:

2 tablespoons butter
2 tablespoons flour
8 ounces beer (one can or bottle of beer)
¼ teaspoon cayenne pepper
¼ teaspoon paprika
Salt and pepper to taste

Directions:

In a small Dutch oven, heat oil. Lightly flour and season the pork chops with salt, pepper paprika, and brown them on each side for 3 minutes per side. Remove chops from the Dutch oven, cover with foil and set aside. In Dutch oven add garlic and onion and sauté for 3-4 minutes until the onion becomes soft. Then add apples and cook over medium heat for about 4 minutes or until the apples begin to soften. Place the chops and their juices over the onion and apple mixture and set aside while making the sauce. Make your sauce by melting butter in a sauce pan. Whisk in the flour and cook for about 1 minute over medium heat. Slowly whisk in the beer to make the sauce. Add salt, pepper, paprika and cayenne pepper and let come to a boil. Remove from heat and pour over the pork chops. Cover and place the Dutch oven in a preheated 350-degree oven and bake for 45 minutes until the chops are fork tender.

Rusyn Beef Roulades

Many Carpatho-Rusyns immigrated to southwestern Pennsylvania. This Pittsburgh specialty was created by a local chef to honor Gregory Zatkovich, a Pittsburgh attorney who worked diligently to have Carpatho-Rusyns recognized as a distinct nationality with political independence. Zatkovich became the first Governor of Carpathian Ruthenia.

Ingredients:

2 pounds of top sirloin steak cut into 6
   portions, pounded or cut very thin to
   about ⅛-inch thick for a roulade
2 cups potatoes, diced small
1 cup ham, diced small
1 teaspoon Dijon mustard
½ cup parsley, chopped
2 teaspoons fresh thyme
1 large onion, chopped
1 leek, chopped (white and light green part)
1 parsnip, diced
1 carrot, diced
1 cup red wine
1 cup beef broth
1 cup sour cream
1 tablespoon flour
Salt and pepper to taste
2-3 tablespoons butter and oil

Directions:

Prepare roulade filling by combining potatoes, ham, mustard, 2 teaspoons parsley, 1 teaspoon thyme, and salt and pepper. Season each roulade with salt and pepper then spread the filling mixture over each beef slice. Roll up each roulade and secure with string or a skewer.

In a Dutch oven, heat 2-3 tablespoons of butter and oil. Add roulades and brown over medium high heat on all sides. Remove meat from the Dutch oven

and set aside. Add onions, leek, carrot and parsnip and sauté for 3 minutes. Return the roulades to the Dutch oven with all its juices, beef broth, wine, and the remaining thyme and parsley, and salt and pepper. Cover and simmer for 2 hours. After that time remove the roulades and set aside. Remove the vegetables and puree them using a food processor or blender to make the sauce. Return the puree back into the Dutch oven. Mix the sour cream with flour, then add sour cream mixture to the puree mixture to thicken the sauce. Stir the mixture well. Add the meat and let simmer about 10 minutes. To serve, place roulades and sauce over buttered noodles.

Kielbasa Stewed with Tomatoes and Vegetables

This is a really good one pot meal that goes well served over white rice. I especially like to make it during the summer months when the vegetables are at their peak. For smaller portions, this recipe can be cut in half and other vegetables can be added such as green beans, eggplant or cauliflower.

Ingredients:

1 pound kielbasa cut into one-inch round slices

1 large onion (2 cups), chopped

2 cloves garlic, chopped

4 ounces fresh mushrooms, sliced thick

½ head white cabbage (about 4-6 cups), cut in about 2-inch pieces

2 small zucchini (about 4 cups), cut into 1 inch thick rounds or cubes

1-2 Hungarian banana hot peppers with the tops and seeds removed, cut into 2-inch pieces (optional)

2 cans (28 oz.) pear shaped tomatoes with juice, cut or break up tomatoes

2 tablespoons olive oil

Salt and pepper to taste

2 tablespoons of parsley, chopped

Directions:

In a pot add oil, garlic and onion and sauté for 3 minutes over medium heat. Add cabbage and cook for about 20 minutes until the cabbage is almost tender. Add tomatoes with their juice and the zucchini, kielbasa, hot pepper and let simmer for about 20 minutes, then add mushrooms and parsley. Simmer another 10 minutes until the vegetables are soft.

Kulebiak

Kulebiak is a native Polish dish that literally means "fingers" because of its shape. Traditionally, it consists of yeast bread filled with meat, fish or vegetable mixtures. Every country, if you think about it, has a version—Italy has its calzones, France has its *tourte*, the Middle Eastern countries have meat and spinach pies, Cuba, Puerto Rico and other Hispanic countries love their empanadas, even America has its commercial "hot pockets." But the Polish version has taken it to a higher level on the gastronomic chart. My grandmother made *kulebiaks* when she baked homemade bread and had dough left over. They were filled with whatever she had available but the combinations are limitless.

For an elegant but easy version, I adapted this concept using puff pastry.

Note: The classic recipe uses chopped hard boiled eggs for the top layer of the salmon. However, I prefer the taste and look of the putting the rice and spinach mixture on the top and bottom of the fish.

Ingredients:

1 large onion, chopped
6-8 cups fresh spinach, chopped
3 tablespoons butter
1 cup <u>cooked</u> white long grain rice
1 piece of salmon about 14-18 ounces,
   bottom skin removed
1 tablespoon fresh lemon juice
2 tablespoons fresh dill, chopped
3 hard-boiled eggs chopped (Optional)
2 puff pastry sheets defrosted (one box)
Salt and pepper to taste
1 beaten egg (for egg wash)
Parchment paper for baking

Directions:

Step #1

Melt butter in a medium size skillet and add onions. Cook for about 4 minutes, then add spinach and sauté another 4 minutes. When vegetables are soft, remove from stove and set aside to cool. When cool add rice, dill, lemon juice and salt and pepper. Mix well to combine and set aside.

Note: I prefer to make this step a day or two in advance because it is easier to work with cold from the refrigerator.

Step #2

Defrost puff pastry according to the package. Working with one sheet at a time, unfold the puff pastry sheets on a lightly floured surface and using a rolling pin, roll sheet to remove creases and accommodate the length of the salmon, leaving about an inch border on the top and bottom of the puff pastry. Transfer the pastry to a baking sheet covered with parchment paper. Place ½ of the spinach-rice mixture on the pastry as a base for the salmon. Remember to leave about an inch border. Place the salmon on top of the rice, then season the salmon with salt and pepper. Brush egg wash around the perimeter of the puff pastry. Place the remaining spinach-rice mixture in top of the salmon, then place the second piece of pastry in top. Press seams together to seal and crimp the seams together. Brush the entire *kulebiak* "finger" with egg wash. Score or decorate (optional) the top with left over pieces of puff pastry, making 3-4 vents to allow the steam to escape. Put the *kulebiak* that was prepared on the parchment paper lined baking sheet in a preheated 400-degree oven for 30-40 minutes until the puff pastry dough is golden. Let *kulebiak* set for about 10 minutes before cutting.

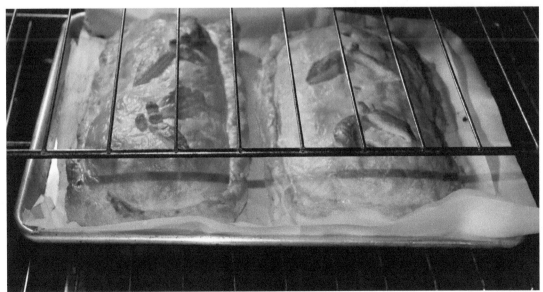

Vegetables and Salads

Mushroom and Rice Cakes with Dill Sauce

Czech Mushroom Strudel

Rina's Summer Vegetable Salad

German Sweet and Sour Braised Red Cabbage with Apples

Ukrainian Stuffed Tomatoes

Barley Salad with Vegetables

Classic Cucumber Salad *Mizeria*

Mom's Potato Pancakes

Stuffed Hot Hungarian Peppers or Tomatoes

Roasted Russian Banana Peppers

Mushroom and Rice Cakes with Dill Sauce

Ingredients for Rice Cakes:

1 pound white button mushrooms, chopped small

2½ cups cooked white rice

6-8 scallions, chopped (include light green part and some green stems)

2 tablespoons parsley, chopped

4 tablespoons butter

1 egg

½ cup flour

Oil for frying the cakes

Salt and pepper to taste

Ingredients for Dill Sauce:

8 teaspoons butter

½ cup flour

3 tablespoons fresh dill, chopped

2 tablespoons fresh lemon juice

2 cups sour cream

1 cup hot water

Salt and pepper to taste

Directions:

Melt butter in a skillet and sauté mushroom and onions on medium heat for about 5-7 minutes. Remove from the stove and let cool. In a large bowl, add rice, mushroom mixture, parsley, seasonings, egg and mix well. Form the mixture into about 12 cakes, lightly coat each cake in flour and place on wax paper. (The cakes can be refrigerated at this point.) Now, heat the oil and fry the cakes on medium heat for about 3 minutes on each side or until golden brown. Remove cakes and let drain on paper towel and keep warm until ready to serve.

Directions for Dill Sauce:

For the dill sauce, make a *zapraska* by melting butter into a small saucepan and whisking in the flour. Cook for about 2 minutes, then add the remaining ingredients. Bring to a boil and cook for about 2-3 minutes. Serve immediately with the mushroom and rice cakes.

Czech Mushroom Strudel

The original recipe used homemade bread dough. It has been adapted using frozen puff pastry. This is a very elegant appetizer, side dish, or a wonderful vegetarian lunch dish.

Ingredients:

1 pound fresh mushrooms, sliced thick (I like to use a variety of two different types: cremini and white button)
2 shallots, finely chopped
2 cloves garlic, finely chopped
2 tablespoons olive oil
2 tablespoons butter
1 tablespoon flour
2 tablespoons each of parsley, dill and thyme, finely chopped
½ package puff pastry (1 sheet unthawed)
Egg for egg wash

Directions:

In a large skillet, using medium heat, add the butter and oil and the garlic and shallots. Sauté for about 2-3 minutes and add mushrooms. Cook mushrooms until tender but do not overly cook because they will bake in the oven. Then add herbs, salt and pepper, and flour. Stir until the mixture thickens. Remove from the stove and let cool completely.

Make the egg wash by beating the egg in a small bowl and adding 1 teaspoon water. Preheat oven to 400 degrees. Working on parchment paper, gently open the unthawed puff pastry and use a rolling pin to remove any creases. Using a pastry brush, paint a two-inch border with the egg wash along the perimeter of the puff pastry. Spoon the mushroom mixture horizontally

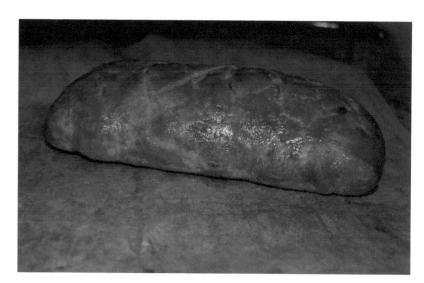

along the longest side of the pastry. You do not want to put the mixture in the center but closer to the edge of the pastry. Then gently lift the pastry to cover the mushroom mixture and seal the edges. Using the parchment paper to assist you, flip the strudel over so all to the seams are underneath. (Note: you can score or decorate the top of the strudel, if you want.) Brush the strudel with the egg wash and make three small slits on the top of the strudel for steam to be released.

Lift the parchment paper with the strudel on to a baking sheet. Bake for 25 minutes until golden brown in a 400-degree preheated oven. Let the strudel rest five minute before cutting.

Rina's Summer Vegetable Salad

Ingredients:

1 pound green beans, stems removed
6 small red bliss/new potatoes
3 beets
2 ripe tomatoes
1 medium red onion, sliced thinly
2 tablespoons fresh dill, chopped
1 red pepper, sliced thinly (optional)
¼ cup fresh lemon juice (or cider vinegar)
½ cup extra virgin olive oil
Salt and coarsely ground pepper to taste

Directions:

To make the dressing, whisk lemon, oil, salt and pepper together until smooth. Set dressing aside.

Wrap beets in foil with salt and a drizzle of olive oil. Place the foil package in a pan and bake for about 30 minutes at 350 degrees until a fork goes into the beets. When tender, remove beets from oven, let cool and remove skins with a knife, then set aside.

Boil green beans and potatoes until tender, then drain well and set aside. Cut potatoes into large bite-sized pieces, tomatoes and beets in wedges. Add all the vegetables together in a bowl. Toss with prepared dressing, salt and pepper, and dill. Serve at room temperature or chilled.

German Sweet and Sour Braised Red Cabbage with Apples

Ingredients:

8 -10 cups red cabbage coarsely cut into 1½ inch slices (about a 2 pound head of cabbage)

1 medium onion, sliced

2 apples (I use Gala or Fuji) cored and cubed, leave the peel on

2 tablespoons vegetable oil

Salt and pepper to taste

⅓ cup apple cider vinegar

1 tablespoon sugar or sugar substitute such as Splenda

2 tablespoons butter (optional)

Directions:

In a Dutch oven or large pot, heat oil and add onion and cabbage. Season with salt and pepper and sauté the mixture for about 20 minutes over medium heat until tender. Then add the apple and cook for an additional 5-10 minutes until the cabbage and apple is tender. In a small cup mix the vinegar and sugar together and stir until the sugar is dissolved. Add the vinegar mixture to the cabbage. (You can add more vinegar and sugar, if you prefer a sweeter/more sour taste.) Let steam for 5 minutes. Remove from heat and add butter. Serve hot or room temperature.

Ukrainian Stuffed Tomatoes

Ingredients:

6 large beefsteak tomatoes

1 pound mushrooms, chopped (include stems)

2 cups cooked rice

1 large onion, chopped

2 cups fresh spinach, chopped or 1 cup defrosted frozen chopped spinach, liquid squeezed out

2 tablespoons fresh dill, chopped

4 tablespoons butter

1 cup sour cream

6 ounces shredded Colby Jack cheese (or your personal favorite)

Salt and pepper to taste

Directions:

Heat butter in pot and add onions. Sauté until translucent, then add mushrooms and sauté for about 5 minutes and then add spinach. Season the vegetables. Do not overcook the vegetables because they will continue cooking in the oven. Set vegetables aside to cool.

Cut the tops off of the tomatoes and scoop out the pulp. (Save the pulp for another use.) Place tomatoes cut side down to drain.

When the mushroom mixture has cooled, add sour cream, rice and dill. Mix well and re-season. Salt the inside of each tomato, then fill each tomato with the mushroom/rice mixture. Arrange tomatoes in a shallow baking dish and top each tomato with shredded cheese. Bake in a 375-degree oven for 30 minutes until the cheese is brown and the tomatoes are tender.

Barley Salad with Vegetables

My mother loved barley and created this salad using any vegetables she had available. Any vegetables, beans or herbs that you like may be substituted.

Ingredients:

1½ cups barley, cooked according to the packaging directions and cooled
1 cup celery, sliced
1 cup red onion, finely chopped
½ cup carrots, shredded
1 cup defrosted frozen peas
1 cup cannellini beans, drained and rinsed from the can
½ cup yellow pepper, chopped
1 cup grape tomatoes, halved
3 tablespoons fresh dill, chopped
1 tablespoon fresh parsley

Dressing:

1 lemon, juice and zest (about 4-5 tablespoons juice)
½ cup olive oil
2 teaspoons grainy-type mustard
Salt and pepper to taste

Directions:

Put all of the ingredients except the dressing in a large bowl. Whisk the dressing together in a separate small bowl, then drizzle over the salad. Mix the salad well, adjusting the seasoning if necessary. Chill for about an hour before serving to let the dressing soak into the barley.

Classic Cucumber Salad *Mizeria*

Although simple, this classic salad goes well with many rich meats and stews.

Ingredients:

1 English cucumber or 8 small pickling
    cucumbers
1 medium onion
1 cup sour cream
1 teaspoon fresh lemon juice
1-2 tablespoons fresh dill, chopped
5 radishes (optional, but really gives the
    salad some color and crunch)
Salt and pepper to taste

Directions:

Thinly slice cucumber in rounds and put into a serving bowl. (If the cucumber is waxed I would recommend peeling.) Next, thinly slice the onion into the bowl with the cucumber, add sour cream, lemon juice, salt and pepper and mix together. Top with dill and thinly sliced radishes and additional cracked pepper.

Mom's Potato Pancakes

Most Eastern European cultures have a version of potato pancakes, the ultimate comfort food! I have fond memories of my mother covering her kitchen counter with "pancakes" draining on paper towel. What a sight to behold! I know you will enjoy this recipe.

Ingredients:

1½ pounds of Idaho or russet potatoes, peeled
½ large onion
1 egg slightly beaten
1 tablespoon flour
¼ cup chopped parsley
Salt and pepper
Oil for frying

Directions:

Grate potatoes and onion together. Drain excess liquid from bowl and add remaining ingredients (except oil). Mix the ingredients well. Into the hot oil, add about ½ cup of potato mixture. With the back of a spoon, flatten the mixture to form a nice round pancake. Fry for about 3-4 minutes until golden brown, then flip and fry on the other side until golden. Repeat until all of your potato mixture is used. Drain pancakes on paper towel and add additional salt. Delicious served hot or warm with applesauce or sour cream.

Stuffed Hot Hungarian Peppers or Tomatoes

The stuffing is great for either peppers or tomatoes.

Ingredients:

12 large Hungarian or banana peppers <u>or</u>
    8 large tomatoes
1 pound Italian-type link sausage
2-3 cloves of garlic, finely chopped
½ cup fresh parsley, chopped
1 tablespoon fresh dill, chopped
¼ loaf of crusty white bread (about 4 slices,
    grinded in a food processor and soaked
    in milk to soften)
½ cup milk
½ cup Parmesan cheese grated
¼ cup olive oil
Salt and pepper to taste

Directions:

Remove the stem and seeds from the peppers and set aside or cut the tops off of the tomatoes and scoop about 1–2 large tablespoons of pulp from each tomato.

In a large skillet, add 2 tablespoons oil and garlic and let cook for 1 minute over medium heat. Be careful not to let the garlic burn. Remove the sausage from its casing and add to the skillet. Break up the sausage with a wooden spoon and cook until the meat is no longer pink. Remove the meat from the stove and let cool. To the cooled meat, add the bread, herbs, cheese and salt and pepper. Mix well.

When the mixture is cool enough to work with, fill the peppers or tomatoes with the meat mixture and arrange in a shallow roasting pan. Drizzle with the remaining oil and salt and pepper. Bake uncovered for about 30 minutes in a 350-degree oven.

Roasted Russian Banana Peppers

A simple and delicious way to cook peppers. My dad's favorite! These peppers are a wonderful accompaniment to any meat or sandwich served on crusty bread.

Ingredients:

2 pounds banana hot peppers (stems and seeds removed and sliced in half from the top of the pepper to the end)
4 cloves garlic, sliced
1 cup olive oil
2 teaspoons dried Italian seasoning or dried oregano
Salt to taste

Directions:

Arrange peppers in a shallow roasting pan, add oil, garlic, salt, and seasoning. Bake in a 400-degree oven for 30 minutes until brown and tender.

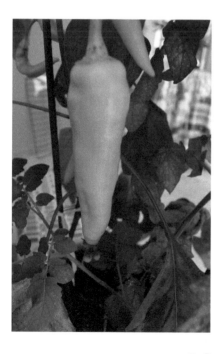

Desserts

Babka Wielkanocna

Austrian Sour Cream Pound Cake

Mom's Slovak Cake

Poached Pears in Wine

Cheese Pocket *Kolache/Kolaczki*

Spiced Glazed Fruit Compote

Russian Tea Cakes

Aunt Norma's Spice Cake

Rustic Plum Tart

Lekvar

Plum Cake (upside down cake) *Placek ze Sliwkami*

Kolache /Kolaczki

Long Nut Roll *Kolache/Kolaczki*

Aunt Katie's *Mazurka*

Babka Wielkanocna

Babka is a Polish coffee cake, very similar to the now commercialized Italian Panettone. *Baba* in Polish means "old woman" or "grandmother" and the coffee cake which is traditionally made in a fluted pan resembles an old woman's full skirt.

Ingredients:

1½ cups whole milk, scalded
6½ cups all purpose flour
2 packages dry active yeast
¼ cup lukewarm water
1 cup granulated sugar
1 teaspoon salt
6 eggs beaten well
1 teaspoon vanilla extract
½ teaspoon almond extract
1 cup butter, at room temperature
2 teaspoon orange zest
2 teaspoon lemon zest
1 cup golden raisins soaked in rum

Directions:

Pour the scalded milk in a bowl and set aside. Dissolve the yeast packets in lukewarm water and let stand for 5 minutes. Beat butter and sugar until fluffy. Add eggs one at a time until well blended. Add yeast mixture, salt, vanilla and almond extracts, and the lemon and orange zest. Mix well and then add the flour alternately with the milk until a soft dough forms. Stir in raisins and knead dough for 10 minutes. Cover and let rise in a warm place for about 1 hour until double in size. Punch down and let rise again.

Generously butter a 12-inch fluted pan. Punch down the dough and put into the prepared pan. Let rise for about an hour or until the dough fills the pan.

Bake at 350 degrees for 25 minutes and lower the heat to 250 degrees and bake 25 minutes more. Remove *Babka* from the oven and let cool for about 5 minutes. Then remove from the pan onto a wire rack to cool. When completely cool, sprinkle with the traditional powdered sugar or a thin icing glaze.

Austrian Sour Cream Pound Cake

The best pound cake that you will ever eat! It goes well with summer fruits such as strawberries, raspberries and blackberries with a dollop of "Polish whipped cream."

Ingredients:

3 cups sugar

3 sticks butter

6 eggs

3 cups cake flour

¼ teaspoon salt

¼ teaspoon baking soda

8 ounces sour cream

2 teaspoon vanilla

¼ cup powdered sugar for dusting

Directions:

Cream butter and sugar until fluffy, and add eggs one at a time. Add flour, one cup at a time until well blended. Mix the baking soda to sour cream and then add sour cream mixture to the batter blending well. Add salt and vanilla and mix well. Pour into a well greased tube pan. Bake at 350 degrees for 55-60 minutes. After cake cools or before serving, dust with powdered sugar.

Polish Whipped Cream

Ingredients:

16 ounces sour cream

1 cup sugar

1 8-ounce container frozen whipped topping, such as Cool Whip

Directions:

In a medium size bowl, add sugar to sour cream and let sit for about 15 minutes until the sugar dissolves. Fold in the defrosted frozen whipped topping into the sour cream mixture. Refrigerate until ready to serve.

Mom's Slovak Cake

For Christmas, my mother would often make nut and apricot *kolache*. She often made extra nut and apricot filling that could be refrigerated and used in this cake which was enjoyed on New Year's Day. What a delicious way to begin the New Year!

Ingredients for dough:

5 cups flour

1¼ cups sugar

3 teaspoons baking powder

½ teaspoon salt

1 cup Crisco

2 eggs, slightly beaten

1 cup sour cream

2 teaspoons vanilla

Ingredients for pineapple layer:

1 - 20-ounce can crushed pineapple with juice

2½ tablespoons cornstarch

¾ cup sugar

2 eggs, lightly beaten

½ teaspoon vanilla

1 tablespoon butter

Ingredients for nut layer:

2 cups walnuts, ground

1 cup sugar

¼ cup whole milk

½ stick butter, melted

Ingredients for apricot layer mixture:

2 cups apricot *lekvar* filling (homemade or store bought)

Directions:

Step #1: First make the three fillings: pineapple, nut and apricot.

For the pineapple filling add all of the ingredients in a sauce pan and cook over medium heat until the mixture thickens. Set aside and let cool.

For the nut filling add all of the ingredients together blending well. Set aside.

For the apricot filling, please see recipe for apricot *lekvar* on page 17 or purchase it in a can.

Step #2: To make the dough add all of the dry ingredients: flour, sugar, baking powder, and salt in a large bowl. Then cut in the Crisco as you would for pie crust. (I use a mixer.) Mix in eggs, sour cream, and vanilla. Blend well to form the dough. Divide the dough into 4 equal parts, form each ball into a disc, cover with plastic wrap and refrigerate for 10-15 minutes.

Step #3: Assemble the "cake" by rolling out one ball of dough between two pieces of waxed paper to fit a greased 13 x 9 inch pan. Place the dough in the pan and top with the nut mixture. Roll the second ball of dough and place on top of the nut mixture and top with the pineapple mixture. Repeat this process and top the third piece of dough with the apricot filling. Roll the final ball of dough and cut into 1-inch strips to lattice the top of the cake. Note: Refrigerate the dough if you are having difficulty in rolling. Place the strips about ½-inch apart, lattice style on top of the apricot filling. Bake in a pre-heated 350-degree oven for about 45 minutes.

Poached Pears in Wine

For those at Christmas who enjoy a lighter and perhaps a "healthier" dessert, this comes highly recommended.

Ingredients:

6 ripe but firm pears (I use the Bosc or
   Bartlett varieties)
4 cups of a fruity red wine (or 1 bottle)
1 cup granulated sugar
2 cinnamon sticks

Directions:

Put wine in a pot with sugar and cinnamon stick. Over medium heat bring to a slow boil or simmer until the sugar dissolves. Reduce heat to a simmer once sugar is dissolved.

Meanwhile, carefully peel the pears, leaving the stems intact. Add pears to wine and poach at a very low simmer for about 7-10 minutes. Carefully turn pears so they absorb the wine on all sides and turn color. When tender, remove pot from stove and let pears cool in the wine mixture. Remove cinnamon stick from wine and discard. Transfer pears to a storage

plastic container or serving bowl. Boil the wine mixture on medium heat until it reduces by half and becomes syrupy. Then let wine cool and add to the pears. Let the pears marinate in the wine liquid at least 24 hours. Serve the pears with the wine sauce. A side of vanilla ice cream goes well with the pear.

Cheese Pocket *Kolache/Kolaczki*

This *kolache* is my Czech paternal grandmother's recipe and my father's favorite holiday sweet as a child. On a farm with numerous cows, cottage cheese was always abundant. The cottage cheese was sweetened and used as a filling for this yeast dough. If you don't like cottage cheese, *lekvar*, apricot or poppy seed can be substituted to fill this *kolache*. At Easter this *kolache* is very popular in my family. It is very similar to cheese Danish and goes well with coffee for breakfast.

Recipe for Cottage Cheese Filling

Ingredients:

1 pound creamed cottage cheese
1 egg yolk (well beaten)
8 ounces Philadelphia Cream Cheese (room temperature)
1 cup sugar
4 tablespoons Tapioca
1 teaspoon vanilla
Zest of 1 lemon or 1 cup well drained crushed pineapple (optional)

Directions:

First make the cheese filling since it needs to rest for two hours. Using a fork, beat the cream cheese until smooth and then add the sugar. Mix in the remaining ingredients and set aside to rest in the refrigerator for two hours.

Recipe for the Dough

Ingredients:

1 cup whole milk
4 cups all purpose flour
1 package dry yeast
1 teaspoon salt
½ cup butter
2 eggs (well beaten)
¼ cup granulated sugar
1 teaspoon vanilla

Directions:

In your mixer bowl add flour and yeast, set aside. In a saucepan, heat milk, butter, sugar, and salt until the mixture is warm and the butter melts. Pour the milk mixture into the flour mixture, add the eggs and vanilla and beat for about 3 minutes using an electric mixer on medium speed. The dough will be sticky. Turn the dough onto a floured board and knead for about 5 minutes adding a little flour to prevent sticking to your board.

(Note: the dough will still be a little sticky at this point but after it rises it is actually a very nice dough to work with.)

Place dough in a greased bowl, cover, and let rise in a warm place for about 1 hour until doubled in size.

Punch down the dough and divide in half. After the dough rests for 10 minutes begin rolling the dough, rather thin because it will rise again, into a rectangle shape. Cut the dough into 4 x 4 inch squares. Fill each square with 1-2 teaspoons of filling in the center. Brush each corner with water and then overlap the four corners together and gently press to ensure that they stick together. Place on a greased baking pan, cover and let rise for about 15-20 minutes. Repeat the process with the remaining dough. Bake at 375 degrees for about 15 minutes until golden. Cool on a wire rack and dust with powdered sugar. This recipe makes about 16 *kolache* pockets.

Spiced Glazed Fruit Compote

This is an old family recipe prepared during the Christmas holidays when fresh fruits were not available.

Ingredients:

1 can of each of the following fruits: Pears, peaches, figs, apricots, pineapple, cherries (Royal Anne or Bing), mandarin oranges
4 cups cranberry apple juice
8 whole cloves
2 cinnamon sticks
2 envelopes of unflavored gelatin

Directions:

Drain all fruit and arrange in a decorative shallow dish. In sauce pan combine 3½ cups of cranberry apple juice, cinnamon stick and the cloves. Bring to a boil and let simmer for 3 minutes.

Soften unflavored gelatin in ½ cup of cold cranberry apple juice then add to the hot juice and dissolve. Remove the cinnamon stick and pour the liquid over the fruit and refrigerate to gel. Serve chilled.

Russian Tea Cakes

Ingredients:

1 cup unsalted butter
2¼ cups all purpose flour
¼ teaspoon salt
½ cup powdered sugar
1 teaspoon vanilla
¾ cup coarsely chopped walnuts
3-4 cups powdered sugar for rolling balls

Directions:

In a mixing bowl beat butter, sugar and vanilla. Gradually add flour and salt mixture and beat until well blended. Finally add nuts and mix until they are incorporated throughout the dough. Form dough into 1- to 1½-inch balls and place on an ungreased baking sheet. Bake in a preheated 375-degree oven for 10 to 12 minutes. Cookies should not brown.

Place remaining powdered sugar (3–4 cups) in a shallow pan. After the cookies come out of the oven, let cool for two or three minutes and then while very hot carefully roll them in the powdered sugar, one at a time. (This forms the wonderful coating on the cookies.) Place cookies on a cooling rack and when cool roll in the powdered sugar again. This recipe makes about 3 dozen tea cakes.

Aunt Norma's Spice Cake

This rustic spice cake is has a secret ingredient (prunes) that makes this cake fantastically moist and delicious.

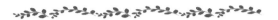

Cake Ingredients:

1½ cup sugar
1 cup Wesson oil
3 eggs (well beaten)
2 cups flour
1 teaspoon salt
1 teaspoon vanilla
1 teaspoon baking soda
1 teaspoon of each: nutmeg, cinnamon, allspice
1 cup buttermilk
1 cup chopped walnuts
1 cup prunes (pitted and cooked)

Directions:

Beat sugar, oil, and eggs until fluffy. Add dry ingredients then buttermilk and mix until well blended. Add prunes, vanilla, and nuts and mix well. Pour batter into a greased and floured 9 x 13 inch pan. Bake at 300 degrees for 1 hour. While cake is hot, use a fork to prick holes over the entire surface of the cake. Spoon the hot sauce over the cake.

Sauce Ingredients:

1 cup sugar
½ cup buttermilk
½ teaspoon soda
½ cup butter
2 teaspoon vanilla

Directions for Sauce:

Put all of the ingredients in a saucepan and bring to a boil. Let mixture boil for 1 minute, stir only once. Remove from stove and wait until the foam goes down and spoon over the hot cake. Let the mixture seep into the cake. Serve with whipped cream.

Plum Recipes

In Poland as well as Pennsylvania, Poles grew plum trees (both Italian prune-type plums and black plums) and loved the fruit to not only eat fresh but to also use for desserts, *lekvar* and preserves. Many plum recipes are included in this book.

Rustic Plum Tart

My grandmother often used her plum preserves in this tart when the fresh fruit was not available. What makes this dessert so special is the crust that contains cream cheese. I have adapted this recipe without her preserves, using fresh fruit and pre-made refrigerated pie crust. It is wonderful and quite simple. But for those special occasions, I've included the recipe for the rich cream cheese crust.

Ingredients for the Crust:

4 ounces cream cheese, room temperature
1½ sticks butter, room temperature
1½ cups flour
¼ teaspoon salt
About ½ cup powdered sugar and ½ cup
    granulated sugar for rolling the dough
Egg wash

OR use 1 pre-made refrigerated pie crust
    (Optional)

Ingredients for Tart Filing:

1½ pound black plums (6-8 large plums), pitted and
    cut into 8 slices
½ cup sugar
1 tablespoon flour for thickening

Directions:

Using a mixer, beat butter and cream cheese and then gradually add the flour and salt mixing until just combined. Form the dough into a ball, wrap in plastic wrap and refrigerate for at least 1 hour.

If using a pre-made pie crust, this step can be eliminated.

Meanwhile, sprinkle sugar and flour over the sliced plums. Line a baking sheet with parchment paper and work right on the parchment paper and even bake the tart on it. Roll the dough into a circle about 12 inches in diameter and ¼ inch thick on a board that has been dusted with granulated and powdered sugars. Arrange plums on the dough leaving at least a two-three inch border then fold the border up and over the fruit filling. Brush the crust with the egg wash and sprinkle with granulated sugar. Bake in a pre-heated 375-degree oven for about 15 minutes, then turn the temperature to 350 degrees and continue baking for about 30 minutes until the crust is golden. Lift the parchment paper holding the tart onto a cooling rack and let cool before transferring to a serving plate.

Note: If you are using a pre-made refrigerated pie crust, use the same process and oven temperature.

Lekvar

Most Eastern European households made *lekvar* in the fall when the fruits were ripe and abundant. If you are wondering "what is *lekvar*," it is fruit that is cooked slowly until thickened to the consistency of thick jam or fruit puree. A variety of fruits can be used for *lekvar* including apricots, peaches and plums. Depending on its use, sugar may be added to the fresh fruits. It was commonly used in our home for pastries such as mazurkas, and *kolache*, as well as *pieroghi*.

It is simple to make, more economical than commercial brands, and the flavor is intense. I feel if you are going to take the time to make your special recipes, it is worth your effort to make *lekvar*.

Ingredients:

5 pounds ripe plums, washed, pitted and
    quartered
2 cups sugar, depending on the sweetness of
    the fruit

Fresh Plum *Lekvar*

Directions:

Using a food processor (the original recipe called for a food grinder), pulse the fruit for about 10 seconds. You will need to do this in batches. Drain any excess juice and put the drained fruit in a large roaster. Bake at 250 degrees for about two hours, stirring occasionally. Then add sugar and cook for about another hour until the fruit is very thick. (Taste and add more sugar, if needed.) *Lekvar* may be stored in canning jars or in plastic containers.

Dried Apricot or Prune *Lekvar*

Directions:

Coarsely cut one pound of dried apricots or prunes, place in saucepan and soak for a few hours in about 1½-2 cups of water. Cook over medium heat, stirring frequently until the fruit becomes soft and somewhat melts. Add more water as needed. Depending on the use of your *lekvar* add about 1 cup of granulated sugar. Stir until smooth.

Plum Cake (upside down cake) *Placek ze Sliwkami*

What makes this cake unique is that it is a true upside down cake. Most recipes place the plums on top of the batter. This cake is really beautiful, simple to make, and good to eat. I have taken a shortcut using a commercial cake mix which is almost as good. But I have also included my mother's cake recipe.

Ingredients:
20 Italian plums pitted
½ cup sugar
½ cup water
½ cup light brown sugar
½ cup softened butter
1 box white or yellow cake mix
1 teaspoon almond extract
1 teaspoon vanilla

Directions:

Place the pitted plums in a sauce pan with water and sugar. Simmer for about 3 minutes until they become soft but not falling apart. Mix together the butter and sugar as you would for a streusel type topping. When the butter and sugar are combined, sprinkle on the bottom of a well greased (with butter) 10-inch cake pan. Arrange the plums in an attractive design, add all of the juice, and set aside.

Prepare the cake batter according to the box and add the almond extract. Pour the cake batter over the plums, and bake at 350 degrees for 35-40 minutes. Let cake cool for 5 minutes and invert onto a serving plate carefully so the plums are not disturbed.

Ingredients for Homemade Cake:
2⅓ cups all purpose flour
½ teaspoon salt
2½ teaspoon baking powder
1 cup sugar
8 tablespoon butter, softened (1 stick)
3 large eggs
⅓ cup sour cream
¾ cup milk
1 teaspoon vanilla
1 teaspoon almond extract

Directions:

Cream the butter and sugar using an electric mixer until fluffy. Add eggs, one at a time, and sour cream, almond extract and vanilla. Add dry ingredients that have been sifted alternately with milk until just combined. Pour over the plums as explained above and bake.

Kolache /Kolaczki

There is a debate as to what truly is "*kolache*"? As the spelling of this Slavic pastry varies by ethnic region, also does the dough and fillings that were introduced by Eastern European immigrants. Traditionally *kolache* constitutes various fillings such as sweet cheese, nut, apricot, prune, poppy seed, or preserves wrapped in different types of sweet pastry dough that may or may not include yeast. My family made several types of the revered filled rolls and they were all referred to generically as *kolache*. Different types of *kolache* were prepared for different holidays or special occasions. There was not a wedding or baby shower, First Communion party, or a special occasion or holiday where *kolache* was not the centerpiece of the desserts. If I were to name "the one" beloved dessert from the "old country" that is a universal favorite among all Poles and other eastern European cultures, it is definitely the beloved *kolache*.

Throughout this cookbook, I have included several authentic varieties for you to enjoy!

In the **Christmas section** (page 6) you will find two types of *kolache*: a small cookie-type pastry made with cream cheese dough rather than yeast; and *povitica*, a very thinly rolled yeast dough that is filled with a variety of different fillings and baked to create a unique swirled design.

Cheese *kolache* that is not rolled in the jelly roll fashion but filled with sweetened cottage cheese and then cut with a criss-cross design can be found in the **Easter section** (page 23).

Czech pocket-type *kolache* resembling a Danish pastry is a yeast dough cut in a square and filled, as in the **Dessert section** (page 73).

Traditional "long roll" type *kolache*, in the **Dessert section,** is a yeast dough usually filled with poppyseed, nut or apricot fillings and rolled in a jelly roll fashion. When this roll is sliced it shows the beautiful pinwheel design of the filling.

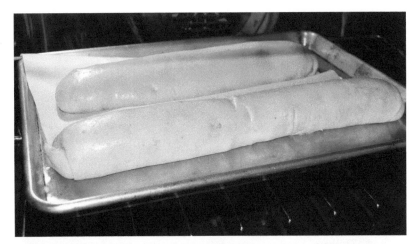

Long Nut Roll *Kolache/Kolaczki*

Note: You can also fill the rolls with poppyseed or apricot filling.

Dough Ingredients:

1 package of dry yeast
2 tablespoons warm water
½ teaspoon sugar
½ cup butter
4 tablespoons sugar
3 eggs beaten
3-3½ cups flour
1 teaspoon salt
½ cup sour cream

Ingredients:

1 pound ground walnuts
¼ cup butter, melted
½ cup whole milk, heated
1½ cup sugar (more if you like it sweeter)
1 teaspoon vanilla
4 egg whites, beaten stiff

Note: This recipe makes three rolls and I usually triple the nut filling recipe using a pound of nuts per roll.

Directions:

First prepare nut mixture, mix the walnuts and sugar together well. Then add the other ingredients, except the egg whites. Beat the egg white(s) until stiff and fold into the nut mixture to keep the nuts firm. Set aside.

Dissolve the yeast in warm water and sugar, set aside. Cream the butter and sugar until fluffy and add eggs one at a time blending well. Add the yeast mixture and the sour cream by hand to the butter mixture. Work a little flour in at a time until a smooth dough forms. Knead the dough and then divide the dough into three equal balls. (Each ball will make a *kolache*.) Roll each ball to about ¼-inch thickness and spread with nut filling. Transfer to an ungreased baking sheet, brush with egg wash, cover and let rise for 1 hour. Repeat the same process using the other balls of dough. Bake at 350 degrees for 30 minutes. This recipe makes three rolls.

Icing (Optional)

Ingredients:

1 stick butter
½ cup Crisco
1 cup sugar
¾ cup evaporated milk
1 teaspoon vanilla

Directions:

Beat butter and Crisco well, add sugar and beat until fluffy. Gradually add milk and vanilla, beating until well missed. Add icing to rolls and top with chopped nuts.

Aunt Katie's *Mazurka*

Ingredients:

2 sticks butter
3 cups flour (plus ½ cup extra flour for dough to lattice the top)
1 cup sugar
1 teaspoon baking powder
1 teaspoon baking soda
4 egg yolks
½ teaspoon salt
½ cup sour cream
2 cans of cherry pie filling

Directions:

Work the butter and flour with a pastry cutter, then add the remaining ingredients and mix well. Spread ¾ of the dough on an ungreased 10 x 14 inch pan with sides. Top the dough with your filling of choice. In this recipe canned cherry pie filling was used. With remaining dough add enough flour to enable you to roll the dough, then cut in strips to lattice the top of the *mazurka*. Bake in a preheated 350-degree oven for 30 minutes. Let thoroughly cool then dust with powdered sugar. Cut into squares.

About the Author

Myra Gaziano grew up in southwestern Pennsylvania among the rich tapestry of foods, traditions and religious holidays, woven from her Eastern European family and neighbors. First generation immigrant families from Poland, Czechoslovakia, Croatia, Hungary and Russia came to the area to work in the coal mines and steel mills, and they brought with them their ethnic cultures and foods. In the small towns, it was commonplace to see restaurants advertising cabbage and *haluski* specials on Fridays, *pieroghi* and *paska* bread for sale at local churches, and festival advertisements that included hog roasts and polka bands. Wedding menus included traditional ethnic dishes and cookie trays displaying the beloved nut and apricot *kolache* for dessert, while guests lined up for the traditional Polish Bridal Dance.

Although not a chef by profession, she was inspired to compile this cookbook to preserve and share the "old-world" heritage of her ancestors. Over the years, the author enhanced her passion for cooking through classes in Florence, Rome, New York and Pittsburgh. She is an alumna of West Virginia University and now lives in Lake Mary, Florida.

Kon Studio Photography

CPSIA information can be obtained
at www.ICGtesting.com
Printed in the USA
BVHW022254230921
617324BV00002B/33

9 781614 935285